TO THEM THAT PERISH

"TO THEM THAT PERISH"

By

ELIAS DODSON POE, M.A., Th.D.

Pastor, Belmont Baptist Church, Roanoke, Virginia

BROADMAN PRESS

NASHVILLE TENNESSEE

Printed in the United States of America
1000—9-39—3

39,823

TO

NAN TRANTHAM POE

THE BEST FRIEND I HAVE

THE BEST PASTOR'S ASSISTANT I KNOW

THIS BOOK IS

AFFECTIONATELY DEDICATED

CONTENTS

FOREWORD

Paul said: "The preaching of the cross is to them that perish foolishness; but unto us which are saved it is the power of God." In this passage I find the title of this little volume of evangelistic sermons.

Every sermon in this collection is a direct appeal "to them that perish" to put their trust in Christ as their Saviour.

Two years ago my first little volume, *God's Heart-Touch,* came from the press. I am grateful for the many kind expressions of appreciation I have received concerning that offering.

I now send forth this little volume—my messages on some of the great familiar texts of the Bible—with the hope that these sermons may find their way to the hearts of many unconverted friends. Any help to this end will be greatly appreciated.

E. D. POE.

Belmont Baptist Church,
Roanoke, Virginia.

I

NO ROOM FOR JESUS!

He came unto his own, and his own received him not.—JOHN 1: 11.

There was no room for them in the inn.—LUKE 2: 7.

And this is the condemnation, that light is come into the world, and men loved darkness rather than light, because their deeds were evil.—JOHN 3: 19.

There they crucified him.—LUKE 23: 33.

Behold, I stand at the door and knock: if any man hear my voice, and open the door, I will come in to him, and will sup with him, and he with me.—REVELATION 3: 20.

In all these texts we are brought face to face with the world's rejection of Christ. The whole Bible portrays this great theme. But in these texts which I have just read, especially do we see the world's wilful and culpable rejection of the Saviour. In them we see in clear focus the eternal antagonism between light and darkness, between good and evil, between God and Satan.

In the first chapter of John, from which our first text is taken, we have a wonderful exhibition of this antipathy of sinful humanity for God, reaching back to the beginning of the world. He says that the Word, God's Message, had always been coming to men, but most of mankind had not been able to "apprehend" it. God was *speaking* to sinful humanity, but sinful humanity did not hear God. The Divine Message was not *received!*

The writer of Hebrews tells us: "It was little by

little and in different ways that God spoke to our
fathers through the prophets, but in these latter days he
has spoken to us in a Son" (Goodspeed). "The Word,"
God's Message, "became flesh, and dwelt among us,"
John says. But when he was born in Bethlehem, "there
was no room for them in the inn." There was no room
for Mary, and consequently no room for Jesus. How
symbolical that incident was! It foreshadowed all that
followed of the world's rejection of Christ, and the
world's amazing refusal to give him the "pre-eminence"
he so richly deserved.

Our third text summarizes the world's reaction to
Jesus. The divine Saviour "became flesh, and dwelt
among us, (and we beheld his glory)." But despite
his wonderful manifestations of the divine life, "men
loved darkness rather than light," and continued their
hostility towards him, until one day they laid hands on
him, and led him out to a place called Golgotha, and
"there they crucified him." There was no room for
him in the world!

The way the world treated him was enough to break
his heart, and some say that he did literally die of a
broken heart! But, Christ still lives! And in the third
chapter of the Book of Revelation, John gives us a picture of him still loving us, and pleading for a place in
our hearts. He is speaking from heaven, saying, "Behold, I stand at the door and knock: if any man hear
my voice, and open the door, I will come in to him, and
will sup with him, and he with me."

All these texts sound forth the tragic truth that, despite the wonderful love of God that impelled him to
give his only Son for the salvation of the world, sinful

men saw no beauty in him that they should desire him. "He was despised and rejected of men." All this hostile attitude of sinful humanity towards Christ sums itself up in one strangely pathetic exclamation, *"No Room for Jesus!"* As we brood for a little while over these words, let us give expression to our thoughts by considering two questions: First, Why do we refuse to make room in our hearts for Jesus? and, second, Why *should* we make room for him?

I

Why do we refuse to make room in our hearts for Jesus? Why do we refuse to open the door and let him in?

I wonder what answer we have for this question.

First, there may be some who will plead *ignorance*. Some may seek to make excuse for keeping Christ out of their hearts by saying that they do not know for sure that Jesus was all that he claimed to be; and so they couple ignorance and *doubt* in their minds as twin reasons for refusing to have anything to do with Jesus. And so doubt runs into *unbelief,* lack of faith!

My dear friends, if you are refusing to make room in your hearts because you are befogged by such feelings and fears and unbelief, you are back where the people were who lived in the world when Christ was born,—when "there was no room for them in the inn." I am quite sure that when Joseph and Mary sought lodging at the inn of Bethlehem the night of the Lord's birth, and were turned away, it was because the innkeeper was ignorant as to what manner of persons he was turning away, and as to what blessed and heavenly event was impending. The last thing, probably, he ever imagined was that he was taking a part in the sublimest drama ever enacted upon the stage of this planet. But the fact that he was ignorant does not relieve the pathos and the tragedy of that scene!

We must remember, however, that although the innkeeper was ignorant of what was transpiring, he missed his great chance of being the first to welcome the Messiah, and of having the star of hope to shine above his inn, and of having the shepherds and the Wise Men visit him to proclaim his Infant Guest as the long-awaited Messiah! What he did, however, in guiltless ignorance cost him dearly; but what he did in ignorance, everyone here today who closes his heart against Christ, does in wilful and culpable aversion to the Light. Jesus put it all into one of our texts when he said, "And this is the condemnation, that light is come into the world, and men loved darkness rather than light." And he added as the reason for this wilful rejection of the Light: "because their deeds were evil." There are, undoubtedly, some poor souls in the dark corners of the earth who might honestly plead ignorance as a reason for not having Christ in their hearts; but we can hardly believe anybody in this congregation can truthfully say that he does not know enough about Jesus to love him and to trust him as his Saviour!

And what I say about ignorance I say also about doubts and unbelief. Do not close your heart against Christ because you may have some questions in your minds about theology that you cannot answer. I am not pleading for a theological dogma; I am pleading with you to open your hearts to Christ!

In the second place, as we seek to answer the question, Why do we refuse to make room in our hearts for Jesus? some will say, "Well, *I am too busy with temporal affairs.*" While Jesus lived here he found many who made this sort of excuse for not coming into the Kingdom; and most of the reasons made by people then for not coming in were that they were too busy with temporal affairs.

Jesus warned men against making this excuse. In the Parable of the Great Supper, those who were invited, you remember, began to make excuse for not coming. One said he had bought a piece of land, and that he had to go and look it over, and therefore could not come; another said he had bought a yoke of oxen, and that he had to go and try them to see how they worked; and yet another said he had married a wife and that he could not get there. Ah, how many make such excuses for not letting Christ into their hearts! Those men of whom Jesus spoke were typical of all men, and their excuses were typical of all excuses for refusing to accept Christ as their Saviour. Some are too busy with their stores or other kinds of business; others are wrapped up in the care of their hogs and horses and cattle, and others are enslaved to their homes! Your hearts are all cluttered up with these temporal and material affairs! This is nothing new under the sun, but we should remember that it is silly for us to make such excuses for closing our hearts against Christ.

Closely related to those men who refused the invitation to the Great Supper was the Rich Young Ruler who came to Jesus and asked him what he should do to inherit eternal life. Jesus told him what he would have to do: he would have to go and sell all his property and give it to the poor, and *come follow him!* Jesus saw that the great obstacle to salvation in that young man's life was the love of wealth; so he went directly to the point with him. And when the young man heard Jesus say, "Go and sell that thou hast, and give to the poor," "he went away sorrowful." But *he went away;* he went away, even though he did it with a sad heart! Undoubtedly that young man was convinced in his own mind that he should take Jesus at his word; but his heart was filled with the love of the world, and so he turned away and refused to let Jesus have his way with him. And many are doing the same thing today.

Another reason for refusing to make room for Jesus is *the love of sinful pleasure.* In this category of sinful pleasure should be placed carnal sins, all sins of the flesh, all sinful living and social debauchery, which are playing havoc with so many people today. It is a sad, solemn truth that most of the young people today who refuse to let Jesus into their hearts as their Saviour do it because they are harboring known sin in their lives! How often do young people today allow the god of pleasure to rule them so completely that they have no desire to live chaste, clean, wholesome lives! They sell their souls for sinful pleasure!

Millions of young people today seem to have taken the Prodigal Son as their ideal and example. He turned his back upon his father, after getting all the money out of him he could, and went into the far country. He went away thinking that he was going to have a lot of fun, and a good time. He plunged into sinful dissipation—he wanted pleasure. He threw money away in a reckless fashion. He ran with the wild, worldly set, and squandered every cent he had on harlots. But, alas, how disappointing such a life proved to be! He wasted everything in the world that he had that was worth having. Sin brought him to the verge of despair and death. At the depth of his misery, sorrow, destitution, and shame, "he came to himself." He had been bewitched by the devil! And when he came to himself, he did the only thing that was left for him to do: he said, "I will arise and go to my father, and will say unto him, . . . I have sinned." And at that he got up and returned to his father. My sinner friends, that is a picture of all young people who fill their lives with sinful pleasure today. I plead, therefore, with any who are giving their lives to sinful pleasure to come back to God, and let Jesus have his rightful place in your hearts!

Why do we not make room in our hearts for Christ? Well, some others may say: "It is not because I am ignorant of Christ's merits as my Saviour that I refuse to make room in my heart for him; neither is it because I am so occupied with temporal affairs; nor is it because I am set upon sinful pleasure; but my trouble is that I am just *negligent;* I just never have done what I know I should have done. I know I should have let Christ into my heart as my Saviour, but I have simply neglected."

I suppose more of us come under this classification of excuse-makers than any other. Sometime ago, I preached from the confession of King Saul, where he said: "I have played the fool." My subject was, "A Self-confessed Fool." I tried to show how foolish it was for a man to trifle with his soul, how foolish it was for a man to neglect salvation. When I gave the invitation to accept Christ as Saviour, at the close of that sermon, a middle-aged man came down the aisle, and as he took me by the hand, said: *"I have played the fool for thirty years;* now I want to accept Christ as my Saviour. I have felt for thirty years that I should take my stand with Christ; but I have just *neglected to do it!"* Ah, my friends, it is a shame for us to neglect Christ; it is a tragedy for us to keep Christ standing at the door of our hearts, and refuse to open the door, and let him in!

In one of the texts that I read at the beginning of this sermon, the risen, exalted and ever-living Christ speaks from heaven, saying, "Behold, I stand at the door and knock: if any man hear my voice, and open the door, I will come in to him, and will sup with him, and he with me." In that text you have a picture of the infinite long-suffering and patience of Christ, and you hear the infinitely sweet and tender melody of his voice, pleading for admission into your hearts! Holman Hunt painted a wonderful picture portraying this scene of Christ at the door. In that painting we see the door fast shut, with rusted hinges, all overgrown with rank, poisonous weeds which tell how long it has been closed. The Son of man stands there amid night dews and darkness, patiently waiting, with one hand tapping at the door, while in the other he bears a light whose rays, perchance, may flash through some of the cracks of the door into the darkness within. In his face are love repelled, and pity all but wasted; in the touch of his hand are gentleness and authority. That picture suggests the pathos and the tragedy of simply keeping the door of our hearts closed against Christ!

There is one feature of that picture that has been widely remarked upon, and which shows the remarkable insight of the artist, namely: that there is no handle on the outside of the door; and the door is so hinged that it opens from within, outwards. That suggests that if we ever let Christ into our hearts we ourselves must do something: we must rise and open the door and welcome him who knocks, or he will remain forever on the outside. Christ will not knock the door down and force an entrance into our hearts; he comes into those hearts only that welcome him. The door has long been shut with many of us, and some of us have deliberately refused to open it. We have even wished that the Holy Christ would go away and leave us. But marvel of all marvels, Christ, rejected, continues to stand and knock; and spurned, he returns! There are men and women in this community who all their lives have known that Jesus desired their love and confidence, and coveted a place in their hearts, and have steeled themselves against him, while they frittered their lives away in worldliness, and sensuality, and sin. I appeal to you who have kept him outside of your hearts by *neglect* and *procrastination* to open your hearts to him now, and let him come in as your Saviour!

In his *Interpretation of the English Bible,* Dr. B. H. Carroll tells a touching incident connected with the text, "There was no room for them in the inn." Most of you have heard the gospel hymn based upon this text, in which the line occurs, "There is room in my heart for thee, Lord Jesus." Doctor Carroll says that in his choir, when he was pastor of the First Baptist Church, Waco, Texas, there was a young woman, "who could outsing the birds, and especially in singing this song could make the stars sparkle." But she was not a Christian. At a gathering of some of the women of his church, in a home of one of them, she sang "No Room for Jesus" with unusual power. At the close of the song the great preacher leaned over and whispered to her, "My child, you sing it beautifully with your lips, but is there room in your *heart* for the Lord Jesus?" She was instantly convicted of sin, and the next Sunday came forward when the invitation was given, her face radiant with heavenly light, saying with joy and tears: "I have not only given him a room in my heart, but all of it, as his residence forever!" Years afterwards, when she was a happy wife and mother, she was dying. The great pastor was sitting by her bedside, and she recalled the time when she made room in heart for Jesus, and spoke to him, almost the last words she uttered: "He is still in my heart, and he is calling me to a room in his Father's house, that house of many mansions!" My friends, have you made room for Jesus in your hearts? If you have not, I hope you will make room for him tonight!

II

Why should we make room in our hearts for Jesus? Why should we open the door and let him in? This is our second great question. Why should we let him in?

We should make room in our hearts for Jesus because *our salvation depends upon it*. Salvation means a great deal more than "going to heaven when we die." Too many have thought of salvation as nothing more than just the hope of "going to rest" when the burdens and cares of this world are ended; but salvation is that, and a great deal more. Salvation involves the forgiveness of all past sins, deliverance from the penalty of our sins, the breaking of the reign of sin and Satan in our lives, a craving for power to overcome all weaknesses and imperfections in our lives, and a desire to grow more into the likeness of Christ. Until we admit Jesus into our hearts as our Saviour by an act of faith, this great transaction can never take place in our souls, and we can never begin to attain the abundant life that Christ came to give us. Now, we should make room for Christ in our hearts because our own personal salvation depends upon it. If we reject him, we are hopelessly lost and will die in our sins, and go out into eternity lost forever!

We should also make room in our hearts for Jesus because of what his presence in our lives will mean to us in the way of peace, comfort, and re-enforcement in all the circumstances and conditions of our lives here in this present world. We need to let him into our hearts because of the comfort and peace that he alone can give us as we face the baffling mysteries, problems, and battles with which life is so constantly beset.

The Prodigal Son in the far country, wrecked, and all but destroyed by sin, asked himself: "What shall I do?" He brooded over his wretchedness, his defeat, his loneliness, his destitution, and his disillusionment. At the depth of his perplexity and in his own weakness he cried out, "I perish with hunger!" O my friends, was not that the cry of a needy soul for God? Is it not a fact that the one thing that we all need *today*, more than anything else at all, for our own peace of heart and mind, is the power of Christ in our hearts to help us to live!

H. G. Wells voices this need of God and salvation in an eloquent passage at the close of his book, *God the Invisible King*. I read it when the book was first published in the horrible days of the World War. He says:

> Religion is the first thing and the last thing,
> And until a man has found God . . .
> He begins at no beginning, he works to no end.
>
> Life falls into place, only with God,
> Who fights through man against Blind Force,
> And Might and Non-Existence;
>
> Who fights with man against confusion and evil,
> Within us and without,
> Against death in every form;
>
> Who loves us as a great captain loves his men,
> And stands ready to use us
> In his immortal adventure against waste, disorder, cruelty,
>   and vice;
>
> Who is the end, who is the meaning,
> Who is the ONLY KING!

Certainly we need God, and our only way to find him is through Christ; *he is God!* Without him we blunder through the world and back to eternity in the dark!

Jewell E. Matthews has voiced this great need in a beautiful little poem:

There is a deep throb of longing
In my soul
For something I have not;
There's a tugging, a sharp tugging
Within me when I see
Masses of fragrant violets,
Or clumps of dogwood
In the springtime.

That same yearning comes
When I look up
At Christ on the Cross
In a stained church window,
And when I read,
"Be still, and know that I am God"—
Can it be God I am hungry for?

This reminds us of those eternally true words of Augustine: "We are restless, O God, till we rest in Thee." When we let Jesus into our hearts, he brings God, and life, and peace! And how we need all these!

In the next place, when Christ comes into our hearts, he glorifies life for us in our workaday world. For the laboring man there is no friend like the Carpenter of Nazareth; for all who are heavy-laden there is no helper like the sympathizing Saviour, who says: "Come unto me, all ye that labour and are heavy laden, and I will give you rest. Take my yoke upon you, and learn of me; for I am meek and lowly in heart: and ye shall find rest unto your souls. For my yoke is easy, and my burden is light." Who else in all the world can speak such words of cheer and comfort and rest as these? What else can so glorify and sustain our lives as the presence of Christ in our hearts?

Then, we should let him into our hearts as our *Great Leader* in this confused world. He is the "Captain of our Salvation." The world is seething with energy, endurance, enthusiasm, intelligence, imagination, and invention, mingled with national prejudice, pride, fear, greed, selfishness, and hate! All of these, like billows, are rolling over us. We are all driven by the storm and tossed by the tempest. But, like a great lighthouse, Jesus stands serene and effulgent in the dark night and cyclonic storm. We need Jesus for what he will mean to us in guiding us into the haven of peace and safety in the midst of the world's present chaos and darkness.

Then, too, we should let Jesus into our hearts because of what he will mean to us in making our homes the kind of places they should be. I have on my shelves a book entitled, *Home, the Savior of Civilization*. In this book I find this statement: "No fact in history reveals the stupidity of man with such disheartening humiliation as his failure to learn and obey God's laws for the family. . . . If one hundredth part of the time and energy spent by men in the gambling game of money-making were devoted to the building and maintaining of ideal homes, this world would become the Kingdom of God in three generations. . . . Every conceivable agency is pulling fathers and mothers and children away from home."

All of us know something about the forces that are tending toward the breaking up of the home as an institution, and anyone who thinks at all feels that unless something can be done to restore and stabilize family life, civilization will inevitably revert to barbarism. As a preacher of Christ, I am convinced that our only

hope in this matter is Christ. Our only way to save
and improve our homes is for husbands and wives to
take Christ into their hearts and lives and make his will
the law of their homes. Our homes can never be better
than the people who live in them.

It is most impressive and encouraging in these times
to find young couples who, as they go forth to make
their way through the world, seek the guidance of the
Lord Jesus. Dr. Curtis Lee Laws, in one of his edi-
torials sometime ago, told a story of such a bride and
groom. They asked him to perform the marriage rites,
and then told him they wanted him to dine with them
the first evening they were in their new home. At the
appointed time, Doctor Laws went over, and found the
young couple blissfully busy getting dinner on the
table. He had been their pastor ever since they were
children, and was like a father to them. When they
went into the dining-room, there was a new Bible at
his place. As they were seated, the young people remarked: "Pastor, we did not want to begin our home
without your blessing. We want you to read to us out
of the Bible, and pray that our home may be the kind
of home Christ would have it to be; we want our home
dedicated to the Lord." Doctor Laws said that in dedi-
cating that home, the Lord seemed as near to him as in
any service he had ever performed.

Quite a number of years ago a young pastor went into
a country community to hold a revival meeting. While
there he was asked to go and talk with a tenant farmer
who lived in a shack on the back of a man's plantation.
The young pastor understood that the man was a hard
worker, and that he had a good wife and some bright

little children, but that he was a drunkard, and that half the time his family was at the point of starvation because the man spent all he made for liquor.

With a heart of compassion that young preacher went to see that man. He had to go down the back way through the landlord's farm, and across the creek to one of the most desolate tenant houses in all the community. He found five little children huddled about on the floor of the little log cabin, while the mother was busying herself boiling some black-eyed peas and baking some cornbread for dinner. He talked with the mother a little, and found that she was a Christian, but that she had had so much trouble with her drunken husband that she had almost given up, and had become resigned to her unspeakable lot. Then, he asked her where he could find her husband, and was told that he was plowing near-by in the field; so he decided to go and find him, and see if he could lead him to Christ.

After a short walk through the pine-thicket and around the little clearing, he met the man at the end of the furrow he was plowing, and soon began to tell him his business. He told him about the meeting in progress at the little church up the road, and talked with him about how he needed Christ as his Saviour, and pleaded with him, for his wife's sake, and for his children's sake, and for his own sake, to give his heart to Christ, who alone could save him, and help him to overcome sin, and to be the kind of husband and father that he should be.

The man's heart was touched, and after a prayer together as he stood there between the plow-handles, he promised the preacher to come to the services that night, and *make a public profession of faith in Christ as his Saviour*. That night when the invitation was given that man was the first to walk down the aisle, and give his hand to the preacher; and he was received for baptism.

The meeting closed, and the young preacher went on his way. Fifteen years later that same preacher was invited back to that same little church to hold another meeting. At the close of his first sermon one of the brethren came up to him in a quiet sort of commanding way, and said: "You are going home with me for dinner!—Do you remember me?" The preacher looked at him, and did as most preachers have to do under such circumstances, saying: "Let me see—I think I saw you when I was here before," hedging. Then the brother asked: "Do you remember coming to see me down back of Mr. Jones' place? Do you remember coming down there to talk to a poor drunkard who was nearly starving his wife and children to death?" Then it all came back to the preacher, and he placed him. Then the brother went on: "Well, I'm that poor drunkard you came to see; but I am thankful that from that day till this, life has been different with me; you are going home with me; my wife and children are expecting you, and I told them I was going to bring you back with me."

The preacher wondered. He recalled the destitution and poverty of fifteen years before. He wondered whether he should go. But the man already had his baggage in his hand, and was leading him out to his car, and it was a *nice* automobile. The preacher hardly knew what to do, or say; but he finally remarked: "This is a mighty nice car you are driving!" In a few moments they were riding up into a pretty grove, towards a big white country residence. The preacher was still bewildered; he wondered if they were driving up to the landlord's home, and if they would then walk across the farm to a tenant house;—he didn't know how to act!

But they drove right up to the front door, and the man got out, and taking the preacher's baggage, said: "Get out and come in!" Again the preacher's curiosity had to be satisfied, so he asked with dawning assurance: "Do you mean to tell me this is your house?" to which the man replied: "Yes—this is our home."

By this time they were in the house, and the wife, as happy as an angel from heaven, and looking younger than she did fifteen years before, came forward to greet her guest. Oh, how happy she was! Then the preacher was shown to his room—a beautiful room with all the conveniences of a modern home.

But the climax came when he went down to dinner, and found all those precious little girls, now grown to young womanhood, waiting in the dining-room to meet him and welcome him for a meal at their table. They remembered him, and the time that he came to their house when they lived in the shack across the creek. Oh, what a change fifteen years had wrought! Now they were all grown, beautiful, and active in the church!

As they stood around the table, the father said: "Brother Johnson, 'the Lord hath done great things for us, whereof we are glad!' We feel that you were the best friend that ever came our way; but for your visit fifteen years ago, no telling where we would all have been by now! We love you; lead us in prayer, and ask especially that Jesus may always be the Head of our home; and thank him for what he has already done for us!" The preacher prayed; and that hour was a foretaste of heaven!

My friends, that is what Jesus can do for a poor lost sinner; and that is what Jesus can do to help a man to make a Christian home, if he will only let him!

In conclusion, let me say we should let Jesus into our hearts because he is the only one who can stand by us in life, go with us down through the dark valley of death, and on out with us to the Great Judgment, and welcome us into the Everlasting Kingdom prepared for us from the foundation of the world!

Whatever others may do, I hope nobody here tonight will ever come down to death without Christ! He is the only friend who can go with us down to the dark river and on through the cold waters, all the way across, out on the other side, and on up the shining slopes all the way to the Father's House. He is the only one who can do that! Our friends and loved ones may go with us down to the last moment of life; but as death presses upon us, and clutches our breath, all earthly friends will have to stand back. Death will have his way! The nurse will have to stand back! The doctor will have to stand back! Wife, husband, father, mother, son, daughter—all will have to stand back when death comes! But Jesus is Master of death, and he has assured us that when death overtakes any who have put their trust in him, he will be with them, to take them over to his Father's house!

O. Henry, the famous story-writer, was dying. The nurse thought the end had come, and began lowering the shades of the windows. Opening his eyes, and seeming to understand, he said: *"Let up the shades! I don't want to go home in the dark!"*

Ah, my friends, if we have taken Jesus into our hearts, when we come down to death, we shall not have to go home in the dark! There will be no dark valley; it will all be light! And if Jesus be with us in death, he will be with us in the Judgment. We shall stand, or fall, in the Judgment according as we have rejected or accepted Jesus as our Saviour in this life. If we refuse to make room for him here, he will refuse to make room for us there.

May God help us all to make room in our hearts for Jesus tonight by accepting him right now as our Saviour!

THE SOUL'S GREATEST EXPERIENCE

Jesus answered and said unto him, Verily, verily, I say unto thee, Except a man be born again, he cannot see the kingdom of God.— JOHN 3: 3.

I speak to you tonight about "The Soul's Greatest Experience." We ordinarily call this experience regeneration, or the new birth. Jesus spoke of it as a new birth, and declared that without this new birth we "cannot see the kingdom of God."

So great and so important is this great experience that someone has said: "It were better never to have been born, than not to be born again." Those who have been born only once abide in spiritual death; while those who have been born twice shall never die. So we see at once something of the vast importance of this, the soul's greatest experience.

I desire to think with you about this experience, from the standpoint of Jesus' conversation with Nicodemus, as recorded here in the third chapter of the Gospel of John.

Nicodemus had seen and heard enough about Jesus to become convinced that he was no ordinary man; and coming to him, he said, "We know that thou art a teacher come from God: for no man can do these miracles that thou doest, except God be with him." Nicodemus felt that Jesus could tell him something about religion that he needed to know. For that reason he came to Jesus and, judging from the statement of our text, Nicodemus must have asked him about the way of salvation. It was in answer to that inquiry that Jesus replied, "Verily, verily, I say unto thee, Except a man be born again, he cannot see the kingdom of God."

In that statement Jesus made the new birth the door into the kingdom of God—the one thing absolutely necessary to salvation!

I

As we follow the conversation of Jesus with Nicodemus, we observe, first, that Jesus spoke of salvation in terms of citizenship in the kingdom of God, or as entrance into the kingdom of God.

For many centuries the Jews had cherished the hope of a Messiah, a Deliverer, a Saviour, and the more devout among them were constantly on the watch for his appearing. Nicodemus seems to have felt that maybe Jesus was that long-expected Messiah, for he said: "We know that thou art a teacher come from God: for no man can do these miracles that thou doest, except God be with him." Nicodemus was perfectly sincere in that statement. He knew that no man could do what Jesus was doing apart from the almighty power of God. Nicodemus was interested and, apparently, was on the verge of believing in him.

So Jesus explained to him the way of salvation, and he spoke of it in terms of the kingdom of God. The Jews had thought that God would appear in some catastrophic, apocalyptic fashion, and that the Anointed One, the King, the Holy One, the Prophet, would appear and seize the reins of government, and set up an earthly reign, through which God would wreak vengeance upon the ungodly, and richly reward the faithful Jews. Such was the Jewish conception of the kingdom of God, and of salvation. But Jesus spiritualized and individualized the kingdom of God idea. He adopted the Jewish term, and filled it with a richer, better, universal, and eternal content. "My kingdom is not of this world," he said; by which he dismissed the idea of a political, visible realm altogether, and substituted for it the idea of a moral and spiritual kingdom, not of "meat and drink," but of righteousness and peace and joy in the Holy Ghost. This was Christ's idea of the kingdom of God. It was a kingdom not of this world, founded by worldly means of conquest and violence, but by humility, by service, by deeds of mercy, by suffering, by witness to the truth; and it was not to be ruled by tyranny nor by force, but by love over hearts freely surrendered to the Messiah, Jesus himself, God's Son.

Citizenship in this kingdom—Messiah's kingdom—the kingdom of God—Jesus regarded as the supreme blessedness, and so taught his disciples. He told them, as he told Nicodemus, that the *summum bonum*—the very greatest good a soul can know—is found in being possessed of a life which truly acknowledges God as King. Such a life is so full, so blessed, so rich in all self-realization, so helpful to all who need help, so satisfying for this world and for the world to come, that no greater blessedness can be imagined. So, to find such a life is to find eternal life and eternal salvation.

II

Now this leads us to the question of how one is to enter this kingdom and be saved. Jesus told Nicodemus that no man could enter the kingdom of God—this kingdom we have been describing—without a new birth!

Jesus said to Nicodemus: "Verily, verily, I say unto thee, Except a man be born again, he cannot see the kingdom of God"; and a little further on he said: "Verily, verily, I say unto thee, Except a man be born of water and of the Spirit, he cannot enter into the kingdom of God."

Now what did Jesus mean by these expressions? They were his answer to Nicodemus' question, "How can a man be born when he is old?" and "How can these things be?"

In order to understand these expressions, we must see them in their historical setting.

John the Baptist was sent of God to baptize. He required evidence of repentance of those coming to him to be baptized, saying: "Bring forth therefore fruits worthy of repentance." While John the Baptist "baptized with the baptism of repentance," he did not stop with that. He taught the people "that they should believe on him which should come after him, that is, on Christ Jesus." John was "the voice of one crying in the wilderness, Prepare ye the way of the Lord, make his paths straight." He was the man sent from God "for a witness, to bear witness of the Light, that all men through him might believe." In speaking of his baptism, John said: "I indeed baptize you with water." On the other hand, in speaking of Christ, he said: "But one mightier than I cometh, the latchet of whose shoes I am not worthy to unloose: he shall baptize you with the Holy Ghost and with fire."

John the Baptist had said: "Repent ye; for the kingdom of heaven is at hand." Jesus explained to Nicodemus the way into the kingdom of God, and that way was by a spiritual birth. And that is why he said: "Except a man be born of water and of the Spirit, he cannot enter into the kingdom of God." He was not talking about two things when he made that statement: he was only saying that the great change necessary for entrance into the kingdom of God was a spiritual change, and that that spiritual birth was fittingly pictured in the rite of baptism.

Nicodemus was greatly perplexed by Jesus' statements about the new birth. It seemed a strange doctrine to him. But Jesus suggested to Nicodemus that he should not stumble over the mystery of this great spiritual change. He reminded him first that the spiritual birth into the kingdom of God was like natural birth into the physical world. "That which is born of the flesh is flesh," he said; and "that which is born of the Spirit is spirit." He was reminding Nicodemus that man has two natures, a physical and a spiritual, and that just as we are born into the world by a physical birth, we must be born into the spiritual kingdom by a spiritual birth. This necessity is based upon the fact that man has two natures. "That was not first which is spiritual, but that which is natural; and afterward that which is spiritual. The first man is of the earth, earthy: the second man is the Lord from heaven."

But Nicodemus was still puzzled; and Jesus again exhorted him not to stumble over the mystery of the spiritual birth. Using another illustration, Jesus said: "The wind bloweth where it listeth, and thou hearest the sound thereof, but canst not tell whence it cometh, and whither it goeth: so is every one that is born of the Spirit." That is the way of the new birth: it is a fact, a great and mighty fact, but a mysterious fact. No more mysterious, however, than the blowing of the wind: you hear the sound of it, and you know it is blowing; but you cannot tell "whence it cometh, and whither it goeth." "So is every one that is born of the Spirit."

Now Jesus argues that we should accept the fact of the spiritual birth just as we do the fact of physical birth, and the fact of the wind. We cannot fully understand either of these, but we do not deny them because we do not fully understand them. Just so, he argues, we should accept the fact and reality of the spiritual birth, even though we cannot fully understand the "how" of it.

III

We cannot fully understand the "how" of the new birth; but there are some things we can do, if we will, to bring about this great spiritual change, since we know that God is always ready to save and help all who sincerely call upon him, and since he never demands the impossible from any of his creatures.

But notice, first, how the new birth is *not* brought about. Let us clear away some erroneous notions as to how the new birth is effected.

First, as we have already seen, the new birth is not brought about by baptism. It is distressing that anybody should ever have entertained such a notion. But let us be clear about this matter, and remember that baptism does not effect regeneration. Baptism is only the outward picture and public profession of our faith in Christ, and a picturing of the great spiritual change which ushers the believer into the kingdom of God.

Second, the new birth is not brought about by belonging to any particular race, or class of people, or any organization, even though that organization be the holy church. Such notions are relics of heathenism, or Judaism.

Third, we should remember that this great inner spiritual change is not produced by outward reform, nor by any other sort of externality. This is probably the most common error about the new birth. The new birth is a radical inward change in which the whole nature is renewed in the image of Christ. This change cannot be produced by outward reform.

Plutarch tells of a man who tried to make a dead body stand upright; but when he had done all he could do for the corpse with which he was working, he concluded by saying: *"Deest aliquid intus"*—"There is something lacking inside." Just so, the man, or woman, or boy, or girl who tries to live the kingdom life without a new heart, without the new birth, will find something lacking inside. We must have a new nature before we can stand upright in the kingdom of God.

Far back in my childhood, an older brother of mine found a wild turkey's nest, and conceived the idea of raising a flock of turkeys from those eggs. So he brought them home and set them under one of the most motherly old hens I ever saw. I can never forget the thrill and excitement of the whole family over the prospect of soon having a gang of turkeys about the place.

We could hardly wait for the eggs to hatch. But when they finally began to hatch—behold, they were little wild turkeys! We had not anticipated such a thing! As soon as one was out of the shell, off to the weeds and bushes he would run! They could not be stayed! The terror and dismay of that good old hen at the wild and wayward behavior of her strange, unregenerate brood were pitiful! She nearly killed herself running after and trying to control those little wild turkeys— but to no avail! They were soon gone with the wind! *There was something lacking inside!* The fact that they were hatched by a gentle, motherly, domesticated hen did not change the nature of those little turkeys! They could not live like little chickens because they did not have the nature of little chickens!

Fourth, I remind you that the new birth cannot be attained by hiding, nor by covering up our sins in our hearts. This is an external treatment which does not remove the seeds of death, nor produce a new spiritual life. Many people seem to think that if they can hide their sins they are all right: but they cannot hide them from God!

Just recently I read a story that illustrates this point. A young college woman had a horrible birthmark all over one side of her face. She suffered unspeakably on account of her unfortunate facial blemish. Her parents spent a great deal of money trying to find a surgeon who could remove the mark, but to no avail. Finally, when the young woman had finished college, having studied chemistry, she set to work to produce a covering that would hide her disfigurement and relieve her embarrassment. Finally she succeeded so well that she applied for and received a patent from the United States Government for her preparation. The black-robed judges of the Court of Appeals in Washington sat and gasped in wonder as the young lady daubed cold cream over the left side of her face, and wiped it off with a towel, revealing a hideous, flaming birthmark from her chin to her forehead. Then she applied some of the covering to her face, and added rouge and powder, and in two minutes completely hid her great disfigurement again. Again the judges gasped, so dramatic was the contrast! But the birthmark remained—it was only covered up! My friends, that is a parable of the unregenerate person trying to improve himself in God's sight by hiding his sin in his heart. Covering our sins by outward reform, or by keeping them hidden from the gaze of men, does not hide them from God, who looks on the heart. But none of these performances can ever regenerate the soul; they can never effect one's salvation.

IV

So, let us now note the positive steps one *can* take which will assuredly bring about the new birth. In the first place, we must realize that the new birth is possible for us, if we desire it. Since God does not require the impossible of any of his creatures, we can rest assured that we can be born of the Spirit, if we desire it!

But we must desire it; else we will remain forever strangers to the kingdom of God. But God is always doing all in his power to awaken within us this *holy desire*—this hunger and thirst after righteousness. God loves us and seeks through the Holy Spirit to convict us of sin, and of righteousness, and of the Judgment to come. God so loved us that he gave his only begotten Son to come into the world to die for us, with the hope that such a display of his love would win our love, and draw us back to himself. Then God, through the Holy Spirit, uses truth, and beauty, and all special providences and common blessings to incline our hearts to holiness and to salvation. God was speaking in Christ from heaven when he said, "Behold, I stand at the door and knock: if any man hear my voice, and open the door, I will come in to him, and will sup with him, and he with me." God is infinitely concerned that we should desire to be saved, and has done all that he can do to incline our hearts to life and to salvation in the kingdom of God. I hope, therefore, all here tonight desire to be saved!

Now if you desire to be saved, the next step is easy— it is turning away from sin. Our sins separate us from God; and it is the love of sinning that holds us back from entrance into the kingdom of God. This turning away from sin we call repentance. Of course, if it is true repentance, it is a turning based upon a realization of our wrongness in God's sight, and that we are failing to fulfil God's purpose in our lives. Such a turning is repentance; and we must thus turn away from sin if we are ever to be born into the kingdom of God.

But there is one more step that we must take before God can receive us into his kingdom. That step is called *faith in Christ*. "God so loved the world, that he gave his only begotten Son, that whosoever believeth in him should not perish, but have everlasting life."

Here we see that the way by which we finally appropriate salvation for ourselves is by believing in Christ.

Now what do we mean by believing in Christ? Jesus explained this to Nicodemus. He went back to the Old Testament for an illustration of saving faith. He recalled the incident where the people were bitten by the fiery serpents, and were dying; and where God commanded Moses to make a serpent of brass, and elevate it in the midst of the camp so that all who were bitten could look upon the uplifted serpent and be healed. Then he said to Nicodemus, "As Moses lifted up the serpent in the wilderness, even so must the Son of man be lifted up: that whosoever believeth in him should not perish, but have eternal life." "The viper-bitten Hebrew looked believingly to the brazen serpent uplifted by Moses and was healed; so every envenomed soul must look by faith to the uplifted Lord." If we look in faith we shall be saved!

There is nothing magical about such a faith in Christ. The spiritual world is as real as the material world; and if we trustingly commit ourselves to Christ, we thereby establish a vital union with God. And that is to be born into the kingdom of God—it is to be born of the Spirit—that is to have eternal life!

This is my message to you about the new birth. May God vouchsafe to every one here this great experience! Without it we cannot enter into the kingdom of God. "Verily, verily, I say unto you, Except a man be born again, he cannot see the kingdom of God."

III

"NOT FAR FROM THE KINGDOM"

Thou art not far from the kingdom of God.—MARK 12: 34.

I desire to think with you tonight about this man who was "not far from the kingdom of God."

A group of hostile people had come to Jesus, asking him questions "to catch him in his words." Along with them came the man of our text, a scribe, who was greatly impressed with the wisdom with which Jesus answered his questioners, and he decided that he would ask a question. His question was this: "What is the first commandment of all?"

Jesus answered him: "The first of all commandments is, Hear, O Israel; the Lord our God is one Lord: and thou shalt love the Lord thy God with all thy heart, and with all thy soul, and with all thy mind, and with all thy strength: this is the first commandment. And the second is like, namely this, Thou shalt love thy neighbour as thyself. There is none other commandment greater than these."

The man of our text agreed with Jesus, and replied: "Well, Master, thou hast said the truth. . . . And when Jesus saw that he answered discreetly, he said unto him, Thou are not far from the kingdom of God."

In this incident we are brought face to face with a man who holds his soul in his hand. Before him are all the fateful alternatives of life and death, of time and eternity. He is not far from the kingdom, yet he is not in it. We cannot help from wondering what he will do. Will he go in, or will he turn back? Will he accept Christ and be saved, or will he reject him and be lost? His soul's salvation depends upon his decision.

Feeling confident that there are some here tonight who are "not far from the kingdom of God," and realizing that your choice for eternity may hang upon the decision you may make before you go out from this service, I desire to think with you for a little while about this man,—this man who was "not far from the kingdom of God."

I

As I brood over this man's situation, I am reminded that there are *some who are far from the kingdom*. There are some who are far, *far* from the kingdom of God; some who are full of all sorts of unholiness and antagonisms to Christ. The Bible is full of examples of such people.

The hypocritical Pharisees and Herodians, who were trying to catch Christ in his words, who were asking him all sorts of captious questions simply to find fault with him, were far from the kingdom of God. Jesus was never quite so hopeless of any other people as he was of those who were blinded by prejudice and who were determined not to heed his teachings, who were always hunting for somthing to find fault with. That procession of enemies who came asking him questions, with no desire to be better themselves, but hoping to make trouble for Jesus, were typical of all men everywhere who trump up excuses for not becoming Christians and not following Christ. The man who finds fault with Christ is far from the kingdom of God.

And the Pharisee who came up to the Temple to pray was far from the kingdom of God. He stood and prayed with himself, saying, "God, I thank thee, that I am not as other men are, extortioners, unjust, adulterers, or even as this publican. I fast twice in the week, I give tithes of all that I possess." Christ looked upon that man as "poor and miserable and naked and blind," because he was self-righteous, conceited, unbrotherly, full of pride, and void of any feeling of need for his own soul. He had none of the kingdom qualities— "poor in spirit," "mourning for sin," "meekness," "mercifulness," "hunger and thirst for righteousness." These are kingdom qualities and attitudes; but the praying Pharisee had none of them. Such a man is far from the kingdom of God.

Then there was the rich man who allowed Lazarus to die of starvation and exposure at his very gate, while he himself was clothed in purple and fine linen, and fared sumptuously every day. He was far from the kingdom of God. He was selfish and totally unconcerned about both his duty to God and to man. He was a good animal; he was a one-world man. He cared nothing for spiritual matters; all he cared for was the gratification of his animal appetites. He was a materialist. If he ever gave a thought to religion, to God, to his soul, or to his duty to his neighbors, no mention is made of it in the Bible. Such men are far from the kingdom of God.

And there is another man mentioned in the Bible who was far from the kingdom of God. He was the man Gallio mentioned in Acts 18: 17. People all around him were talking about religion; they were talking about salvation in Christ. But the Bible tells us that "Gallio cared for none of those things." All such matters as God, the soul, salvation, heaven, and hell, and vast eternity—he cared for none of these things! My friends, there are many people today who are exactly like Gallio. Talk to them about the church, and they reply they do not care for the church; talk to them about giving their lives to Christ and living right in the sight of God, and they tell you they care for none of those things. Ask them to attend Sunday school or any of the services of the church, and they reply that they care for none of those things. All such people are far from the kingdom of God.

II

But I am glad that there are *some who are near the kingdom of God,* like the man of our text. I am glad that not all are far from Christ. Jesus said this man about whom we are talking was "not far from the kingdom."

Why did Jesus say this man was "not far from the kingdom of God"? Well, a glance at what this man knew and believed, and at the advantages he had enjoyed, will show why. First, he had spent his life in studying, copying, and teaching the Old Testament. He was a thorough-going monotheist. He believed heartily in the one true God; he was no pagan idolater. He agreed with Christ that the first and greatest commandment is to love God with all one's heart, mind, soul, and strength. He agreed with Christ that the second greatest commandment is to love one's neighbor as oneself. He agreed with Christ that heart religion is more than all burnt offerings and sacrifices. And last, but not least, he agreed with Christ as to the resurrection of the dead and the life everlasting. This is implied from his reaction to the answer that Jesus made to the Sadducees with regard to the resurrection of the dead. Now we know that any man who can go along with Christ in all these matters, and has a desire to do the will of God, is not far from the kingdom.

III

Here, however, we come face to face with an altogether important fact, namely: that *being near the kingdom is not being in the kingdom.* A man may be almost saved, yet be lost. A man may be just outside the gate. There are many today like the man of our text. They have been brought up in a land of Bibles, in Sunday school, in Christian homes, and among Christian people. Naturally they know a great deal about religion. It would be easy for them to step over the line and be saved. But they are not saved. They are near the kingdom, but are not in it. Ah, my dear friends not far from the kingdom of God tonight, it is a terrible thought that you may be so near the kingdom of God— so near Christ and salvation—and not be saved!

IV

Now, my unsaved friends, you who are not far from the kingdom of God, I want to urge you to enter the kingdom tonight. *There are many good reasons why you should do so.*

First, you should enter while you are near, because if you do not enter now you will drift further away. Being near the kingdom is, of necessity, a transitional condition. The soul cannot rest for long in a state of indecision, and those who are near today either will go in, or will sink back into the darkness, and may never come near again. It is a crucial moment, a moment of destiny, with a soul to be almost persuaded to surrender to God, and then harden the heart and stiffen the neck and go farther away from God to keep from entering the kingdom.

Aaron Burr, when he was about nineteen years of age, saw that a decision had to be made between the world and God. He went into the country for a week to consider the matter. He then made a resolution never again to trouble himself about his soul's salvation. From that time he threw himself recklessly into sin, sinking lower and lower into depravity, and finally died an outcast in the country that had signally honored him. What a different story his life might have been if he had entered the kingdom of God when he stood before the gate!

Second, my friends who are near the kingdom of God, you should enter the kingdom now because it is wrong to those who love you for you to stay out. A little while ago I went to comfort a mother whose son was going astray. With sobs and tears she said: "I was praying for him the other night, and in my great distress—because of my love for him and my anxiety about him—I found myself asking God to let me die and go out into eternal night, even to endless hell, if that was the only thing that would turn him from his evil ways, and make him a Christian." Ah, young man, that is the way your Godly mother feels about you! That is the way she feels about her unsaved girls; that is the way all true parents feel towards their children.

Third, you should enter the kingdom while you are near because there are others looking to you for leadership, for guidance. There are some who will follow you, who will go in and be saved, if you will go in! How often have I seen friends agree to give their hearts to Christ at the same time! How often have I seen children follow their parents into the kingdom! And I have seen little children lead their parents into the kingdom!

Some years ago I went to the hospital on Sunday morning to see some patients. As I passed through a large ward, I noticed a screen around a bed, and noticed the shadow of a doctor in there ministering to a young man. Presently the doctor came out, and, recognizing me, said: "I wish you would go in there and speak to that boy—he is dying!" I went behind the screen and spoke to him, and held him by the hand. I soon learned that he was not a Christian, but that he was most humble, even pitiful. I asked him if he desired to be a Christian—if he wanted to be right with God. To all my questions he made, in brief, this reply: "I have had a hard time all my life—my mother died before I could remember—my father was a drunkard—we didn't have much of a home. We moved from place to place—many times I was hungry, cold, and had no bed to sleep in. I always wanted to go to church and do right—If I get well, and can get a job and get me some clothes, I want to go to church and Sunday

school. I want to do better than I have ever done."
Then I ventured another question. I said: "My boy,
in case you should not get well, how do you feel about
it?" I knew that was a big, hard question, and I wondered what he would say. But to my great satisfaction, he replied: "Of course, I do not know much about
how it is going to be—nobody has ever told me much
about it—but I have always wanted to do right, ever
since I was a little boy—and now, I am trusting Christ
as my Saviour, and if I have to go—I think God will
understand, and I think he will be *friendly* to me!" I
could stand no more. I assured him that he was right,
and that God indeed would "be friendly to him," and,
holding him by the hand, I commended him to God, the
Great Friend! I believe he went out to meet God in
peace. But, oh, the tragedy of parents leaving their
children to blunder back to eternity by themselves!
Every parent should do his utmost to introduce Jesus
to his children as their Saviour.

Let me tell you another experience. Back when I
was a mere youth I went to a little country church to
hold a revival meeting. About the third night of the
services a father about fifty years of age was wonderfully converted. He had two sons and a young daughter in the congregation, none of whom was a Christian.
When he came forward to own the Lord as his Saviour,
he was shouting and praising God. As soon as he had
told me that he felt that his sins were forgiven and that
he was saved, he turned around and went back into the
congregation to his older son, shouting: "I am saved,
I am saved; thank the Lord, I am saved!" His son,
a big twenty-two-year-old fellow, was shaking all over

with emotion and his tears were falling like rain in an April shower. His father called out to him: "Son, give your heart to the Lord!" Immediately that son came forward, accepting Christ. By the time he had found a seat at the front, the father was bringing the younger son down the aisle, still shouting: "Praise the Lord; praise the Lord!" By the time I had found a seat for that boy at the front, the father had gone back and found his daughter and was bringing her to the front to confess Christ. All this had been taking place while many others of the congregation were coming forward confessing Christ. It was a remarkable service!

This was before the days of automobiles, when people came to church in wagons and buggies, and on horseback. Brother Nowell's family—that was his name—had come that night in a big wagon. They were all so happy they could not keep from shouting as they drove on back home! As they neared the home they got to thinking of how glad the mother and the old grandmother would be to hear the good news! They were so happy that they all got to shouting again. The mother and grandmother had retired for the night, but when they heard the shouting at the foot of the hill they mistook it for distress cries. They thought the horses had run away and that some member of the family was surely killed. The mother and grandmother got a lantern lighted at last, and came running in their night clothes to see what had happened. By and by, however, the new converts made it clear to them that they were all saved. Then the dear old grandmother, more than eighty years of age, who had been praying for all of them from their birth, and the mother and wife, joined the shouting. They all shouted so loud and long that they alarmed the neighborhood. Presently two of the closest neighbors came hurrying over to see what had happened. They were godly people, and immediately joined in the rejoicing. From midnight till broad daylight they rejoiced and praised God together.

Of course, I did not know what was going on over in that home that night, but next day Brother Nowell told me all about it, and took me home with him for dinner. We spent the greater part of the afternoon going over it all. But all during the years since then I have wondered what would have become of those young people if that father had not first given himself to the Lord. I do not know whether they ever would have entered the kingdom of God or not, if that father had not gone in first. My sinner friends, you parents with children about you, you brothers with brothers and sisters; you friends, you neighbors—all of you have influence over others. You should enter the kingdom because there are others who are looking to you for an example, for leadership. I plead with you to use your influence to lead your friends and kindred to Christ now!

And, finally, I urge you to enter the kingdom while you are near because it is so heart-breakingly tragic to be as near the kingdom as some of you are tonight and then go away and be lost forever! It is a law of our nature that convictions not acted upon will soon die, that truth not followed will fade from our hearts and minds, that impressions resisted are harder to be made again, that obstacles to becoming a Christian increase with passing time, that the longer we linger the stronger the habit of lingering becomes. Because this law is so true, tragically true, I plead with all you who are near the kingdom tonight to come in!

Being near the kingdom will not save you. In the days of Moses, God commanded him to set apart certain cities of refuge to which one who had sinned might flee and be safe from the avenger. But the offender had to get into the city of refuge; being just outside the gate would not save him.

One of my teachers during college days went swimming one summer day. He was out in a canoe, which in some way was capsized in water over his head. He made a frantic effort to swim to land, and got within an arm's length of the shore; but there within three feet of safety and life, his strength failed him and he went down to death! He was young and brilliant, and his funeral was one of the saddest I ever attended. Everybody lamented his death and grieved because he drowned so close to shore. He was not far from shore, but he went down just the same!

The story of the disaster of the *Royal Charter* has been told many times, but it always melts my heart. She was the queen of the seas in her day, long before radio and wireless communication at sea. She had made a triumphant voyage around the world, and had gotten back to Queenstown. From there she was to sail only a short distance to Liverpool, her home port. It was only a short distance, but you recall that the *Royal Charter* never reached Liverpool! Many people had gone down to the wharf—thousands of them—to give her a great welcome. The mayor of the city was there, and many relatives of those who were on the great ship were there to welcome their loved ones home. Bands of music were playing. But the *Royal Charter* never came in! She went down in the night with nearly all on board— so near her home port!

Dr. William M. Taylor, a great preacher in New York, was pastor of a church in Liverpool at that time, and the wife of the first mate of the *Royal Charter* was a member of his church; so it became his sad duty to tell the wife of the first mate about the disaster. Doctor Taylor went to the home and rang the doorbell. The little daughter in the home met him, and exclaimed, "O Doctor Taylor, I thought you were my papa; he is coming home today." The preacher said for a moment he felt like an executioner as he realized what was immediately before him as he entered the home. He found the table spread for breakfast, and the wife of the first mate stepped forward, her face shining, as she said, "Doctor Taylor, this is indeed a happy privilege to see you this morning, and we hope you are going to be able to sit with us at breakfast, as my husband is on the *Royal Charter* and is expected at any moment now."

Doctor Taylor, looking at her for a moment, and steadying himself by holding to a chair, said: "Mrs. Blank, I am sorry to have to tell you that your husband will never come home. The *Royal Charter* went down last night, and your husband is lost." She threw her hands to her head, staggered for a moment, and fell, and as she fell she cried: "O God, so near home—but lost!" It was indeed a heart-breaking experience, yet, my friends, there are some here as near the kingdom as that. I plead with you not to go down so near home!

Two friends, not long ago on a cold winter day, went out into the mountains to a lodge for a hunt. The weather was bitterly cold as evening came on. They built a fire in the lodge house so that when they returned they would find a warm shelter. While they were out that afternoon a frightful blizzard swooped down over the mountains. They were separated one from the other. Darkness overtook them before they could get back to the lodge, and one of them lost his way, while the other with great difficulty reached the house, exhausted and half frozen. The blizzard raged far into the night, and the wind howled through the brush and crags of the mountains. Finally the fortunate one who had gotten back resolved to brave the storm and the night to try to find his friend. He opened the door of the hut, and, lo, there, almost on the doorstep, he found his friend—slumped down dead! He had struggled through the blinding snow, the driving wind and appalling darkness, over cliff and through the brush, to the very door of the warm room that was waiting for him! But he perished just outside the door! Being near did not save him! It was utterly sad to die so close to safety and to life!

> Oh, weary soul, the gate is near,
>   In sin why still abide?
> Both peace and rest are waiting here,
>   And you are just outside.

Forgiveness Jesus will impart—
To save your soul he died;
How can you still offend his heart,
By staying just outside.

The day of life is passing by,
Soon night your soul will hide;
And then "too late" will be your cry,
If you are just outside.

Come in, be free from chains of sin,
Be glad, be satisfied;
Before the tempest breaks, come in,
And leave your past outside.*

My friends, all of you who are "not far from the kingdom of God," I plead with you to come into the kingdom tonight!

---

*(By permission The Rodeheaver Hall-Mack Co.)

IV

THE WAGES OF SIN

The wages of sin is death.—ROMANS 6 : 23.

My message tonight is based on one of the great, familiar texts. Many sermons have been preached from it. It sounds forth the same great truth that we hear in such expressions as "Be sure your sin will find you out," and "Be not deceived; God is not mocked: for whatsoever a man soweth, that shall he also reap." All these texts plainly assure us that we cannot do wrong and get away with it. We will have to collect our wages; and the wages of sin is death.

"The wages of sin is death." In this brief text there are three tremendous words—hard, solid, heavy words—"sin," "wages," and "death." They are all linked together in an unavoidable sequence. Where you find sin you will find the wages of sin; and the wages of sin is spiritual death.

I desire to group our thoughts about these three words tonight—*sin, wages,* and *death*—and I earnestly urge you, unsaved friends, to keep the text in your minds while I am talking to you—"The wages of sin is death."

I

Let us think first of all about *sin.* Someone has said that "Sin is a debt, a burden, a thief, a sickness, a leprosy, a plague, a poison, a serpent, a sting; everything that God hates sin is. It is the sexton that digs man's grave. It is the murderer that destroys his life. It is the strange siren, seated on the rock by the deadly

[58]

pool, who smiles to deceive, sings to lure, kisses to betray, and flings her arms about our neck to leap with us into perdition." This is a horrible picture of sin, but no picture of sin can be overdrawn: the stark horridness and deadliness of sin can never be fully told. The Bible exhausts human language in the effort to show men how hateful sin is to God, and how ruinous it is to man. Notice some of the more common ideas of sin as we find them in the Bible.

The commonest idea of sin presented in the Bible is that sin is "transgression." The underlying idea of transgression is that God has certain bounds within which his people may live and move and have their being, and that so long as they stay within those bounds, they are on safe ground, and are assured of God's loving favor; but when they go beyond those bounds, they become guilty of transgression, and, as a consequence, are out of harmony with God; they have broken God's boundary and have gone over into Satan's territory; they are no longer in God's domain; they have turned traitor to God; they have gone astray; they have "turned every one to his own way."

There is a story that has often been repeated of a man who dreamed that he died and went to Judgment. He was a member of the church, but not much of a Christian. When he came to Judgment, fearing because he had not been faithful to his duty, he was asked whether or not he was one of God's children. He was quick to say he was a child of God. But the Judge replied: "But Death found you on Satan's territory." I have often wondered if there are not many professed Christians who will go to Judgment from Satan's territory. That man had *transgressed;* he had passed over into Satan's domain. He had disobeyed the commandments of God.

Another term used in the Bible to picture sin is the word "iniquity." At the last Judgment, those who will hear their doom pronounced and who will be banished from the presence of Christ will be the "workers of iniquity." There are several Hebrew words in the Bible which are translated by our word "iniquity"; but in general they all seem to signify *moral corruption.*

One who is bent upon doing acts of violence, or committing crime, or hurting and wronging his neighbor, is an iniquitous person. He is unclean, as if he had been befouled with the filth of the gutter, and had never been washed of his uncleanness.

The word "iniquity" occupies a large place in our Bible. It is like a whole nest of vipers, all of different kinds. But they are all serpents, with different markings, but equally poisonous.

In the seventh Psalm we find an illustration of the iniquitous person. There we are told that "God judgeth the righteous," but that he is "angry with the wicked every day." And then we are told that the iniquitous man "hath conceived mischief and brought forth falsehood. . . . He made a pit, and digged it, and is fallen into the ditch which he made. His mischief shall return upon his own head, and his violent dealing shall come down upon his own pate."

Psalm 66: 18 says: "If I regard iniquity in my heart, the Lord will not hear me." If I am dishonest, if I am insincere, if I am treacherous, if I am mischievous in my heart—then I am full of iniquity—I am on the way to falling into the ditch I have intended for others!

The word "iniquity" connotes vanity, folly, mischief, evil desire, perversity, and wrongdoing. In the fourth chapter of the Book of Daniel we find an illustration of all these iniquities. Nebuchadnezzar had a bad dream. He dreamed that he saw a tree in the midst of the earth, high and great. The leaves of it were fair, and the fruit thereof much; the beasts of the field had shadow under it, and the birds of the heavens dwelt in its boughs. He saw in his dream a holy watcher come down from heaven, who cried aloud: "Hew down the tree, and cut off his branches, shake off his leaves, and scatter his fruit: let the beasts get away from under it, and the fowls from his branches."

Then Daniel was called in to interpret that dream. He faced the king, saying, "My lord, the dream be to them that hate thee." Then he told him that the great tree represented him; that the holy watcher was the Most High who was coming to destroy his kingdom. Then Daniel admonished Nebuchadnezzar: "Break off thy sins by righteousness, and thine *iniquities* by shewing mercy to the poor." Here we see a king in the toils of his own iniquity. He was guilty of all sorts of vanity, folly, mischief, evil desire, and perversity. And he paid a dear price for it. He did not break off his sins, and his kingdom departed from him, and he was driven forth from men till he recognized his folly and called upon God to help him.

Another picture of sin is found in the word "wickedness." This word pictures sin as crookedness, double dealing, instability. There are many people whose sins are of this sort. There are many unstable, worthless people in our churches. They never get settled, they are always out of place, or are doing some disgraceful, or shameful thing, or something that is totally wrong, or cherishing some malice, or grudge. All such people are wicked.

Jesus was thinking of this sort of sin when he said that no man could serve two masters. It is a particularly weak and foolish streak in a man's character that makes him think that he can run with the hare and hunt with the hound in anything, to say nothing of church and religion. The man who undertakes such a double role is a wicked man. Jesus was thinking of this sort of sin when he spoke of the fruitless fig tree. He had been coming to find fruit from the tree, and had found none. It was worthless, without utility; hence it was good for nothing but to be rooted up and cast out; it was only "cumbering the ground." He was thinking of this sort of sin when he spoke of the "unfaithful steward," who took his talent and, instead of using it, went and digged a hole in the ground and buried it, and then began to complain that his master was a hard and unjust man. Jesus designated that sort of man as a "wicked and slothful servant." All people like that are wicked. Sin often takes the form of wickedness.

You have heard of the old man who, befuddled by drink, got lost trying to get home. He had been out all night, rambling up and down the alleys and across the gardens of the edge of town where he lived. Finally, about dawn, he saw a light in a house close by, and staggered over to the gate and hailed the occupant of

the house, muttering, "Mister, can you tell me *who* I
am, and *where* I am, and *where* I am going?" That
old man was wicked in two ways—he was out of place,
and had been straggling around all night, and was
getting nowhere. He had lost his identity, his loca-
tion, and his destination! He was completely wicked,
in the Bible sense of the word.

I heard of a man who had a "wicked" dog. That
dog, when he was taken out for a hunt, had a habit of
running everything he got a scent of. If he started
after a fox, he would run the fox till he crossed the
trail of a coon; then he would run the coon till he
crossed the trail of a skunk; then he would take off
after the skunk and run him till he crossed the trail
of a rabbit; then he would run the rabbit till he crossed
the trail of a mouse; then he would run the mouse till
he crossed the trail of a cricket; and then he would
end up by running the cricket into a hole in the ground!
That was a wicked dog! He could not hold to one
track; he wanted to run after everything that roved the
woods. There are a lot of people like that dog; they
don't seem to realize that if they are to be worth anything in the kingdom of God they must be able to stick
to one Master. They can't be running every trail they
smell!

The Children of Israel had one besetting sin that
grieved God—their wicked disposition to go off after
strange gods. Our wickedness today is a modified form
of their instability. We have a lot of people who are
very interested in the church one day and the next day
they are going to all sorts of places and doing all sorts
of things that no Christian ought to do; they are all

steamed up in church work today, and tomorrow they are cold!

These three words, "transgression," "iniquity," and "wickedness," suggest most of the content of sin, though there are many other phases of sin suggested by other words.

II

But let us be sure that all sin pays *wages*. Our text says: "The wages of sin is death." Sin pays *wages;* and if we serve sin we must take our pay. We cannot do wrong and get away with it. The Bible is perfectly clear on that point. When some of the tribes of the Children of Israel did not want to go with the others over the Jordan to help drive out the enemies, Moses remonstrated with them, saying: "Behold, ye have sinned against the Lord: and be sure your sin will find you out." The law of sin and death is written in the very nature of things: the universe is keyed to righteousness. We live in a moral order of things. The man who does wrong is fighting the stars!

Adam and Eve sinned in the Garden of Eden. God had told them that they should die if they disobeyed him. The story of their fall is too familiar to need repeating. But their sin was the symbol of all human experience. They were driven out. They could not escape the consequence of their own disobedience. They lost Paradise!

In the next generation, we see that sin had begun to bring its harvest of sorrow. Cain and Abel, sons of Adam and Eve, had their taste of sin and death. Cain slew his brother, and no sooner had he committed the foul murder than God spoke to him, saying: "Where is Abel thy brother?" Then he lied about it; he said, "I know not." But he could not get away with it. God said: "What hast thou done? the voice of thy brother's blood crieth unto me from the ground." Then God told him how he was cursed with a curse, and how he would have to suffer for his sin, and, in desperation, Cain wailed: "My punishment is greater than I can bear." My friends, he was collecting the wages of his sin! It is a terrible story; but Cain was going through just what every sinner in the world must endure. Sin brings death—a terrible, horrible, lingering death!

At the Paris Exposition in 1867 there was a little oil painting, only about a foot square. The subject of that painting was "Sowing the Tares." The face it portrayed was most hideous; it looked like a demon's. As the poor man sowed the tares, up came serpents and reptiles, crawling up his body; and all about him were woods with wolves and other ravenous beasts prowling in them. The painter had brought together the sowing and the reaping, blotting out the period of growth. It was a vivid picture of just what I am saying. He was sowing sin and was reaping death!

There is a poem by Hood called "The Dream of Eugene Aram." It has been often used to picture the treachery of sin, and the certainty of its wages. Aram murdered a man and cast his body into a "sluggish water, black as the pit itself." Next morning he visited the scene of his crime,

> And sought the black, accursed pool,
>   With a wild, misgiving eye;
> And he saw the dead in the river bed,
>   For the fearless stream was dry.

Then he covered the corpse with a heap of leaves, but a mighty wind swept the woods, leaving his secret bare before the sun.   Then he exclaimed:

> Then down I cast me on my face,
>   And first began to weep;
> For I knew my secret then was one
>   That earth refused to keep,
> Or land or sea, though it should be
>   Ten thousand fathoms deep.

This is just another example of sin and death. We need not try to deceive ourselves; sin pays wages; we can't do wrong and get away with it! The world teems with illustrations of this great truth.

The punishment meted out to the "ancient mariner" who killed the albatross, the bird which the sailors looked upon as the bringer of favorable winds, was that he should wear the dead bird about his neck. So sin hangs its carrion upon us.

On the marble monument erected to the memory of Dr. Samuel Johnson there is represented a touching scene. When he was a lad he was asked by his sick father to take some books to Uttoxeter, and sell them in the market-place. He refused to go. When he was at the peak of his fame, fifty years later, he journeyed to Uttoxeter, and with head uncovered, stood for an hour in a pouring rain upon the very spot where the old book-stall had stood. This is the scene portrayed upon his monument. Penitence procured pardon, but could not remove the memory of his sin, and all during Johnson's life he was collecting the wages of that sin.

III

Now what wages does sin pay? "The wages of sin is death." Death is the fateful check every impenitent sinner gets for his slavery to sin!

But what does "death" as used here mean? In the first place, it means moral and spiritual separation from God, with all its awful consequences. Just as the branch, separated from the vine, dies, man separated from God dies. Most of us have been accustomed to think of spiritual death as something that begins in the future world. But spiritual death begins here and now. Millions now living are already dead! Those who are out of harmony with Christ are dead in trespasses and in sin. Death in this sense is broken relations with God. Physical death means the separation of the soul from the body; spiritual death means the separation of the soul from God; and as the body decays when the soul departs, just so does the whole life of man fall into ruin when man is separated from God.

In our Bibles we read that when God pronounced sentence upon disobedience, he told Adam that in the day he ate of the forbidden fruit he should surely die. The Hebrew idiom here expresses this sentence most vividly. It says: "in the day thou eatest thereof, dying, thou shalt die." This rendering suggests two impressive truths:

It suggests the nature of spiritual dying. People do not die the spiritual death suddenly. They die like old people: old people

> . . . go fearfully;
> Husbanding Life's long-cherished spark,
> Whispering fierce denials of
> The closing dark.
> —Carrie Fall Benson.—*Kaleidograph.*

Victor Hugo says: "The agony of death may be said to meander. It goes, comes, advances toward the grave, and returns toward life. There is some groping in the act of dying."

"Dying, thou shall die." This pictures for us the act of dying spiritually. We see dying people all about us every day. They are breathing, they move about; but they are groping here and there; but they are going down! Life for them is not good. Satan has beguiled them into thinking that life without God is better than life with God, when indeed life without God is worse than death!

Death for the sinner begins here and now. Here and now his foolish heart is darkened; little by little he loses his moral sense; he becomes more and more blind morally; he becomes more and more filthy in body, mind, and spirit; his moral and spiritual leprosy eats deeper and deeper into his soul, until at last all that is left in life for him is to stand and cry: "Unclean! Unclean!" as the lepers were required to do in the time of Christ to warn the passers-by not to come nigh them. This kind of existence is the Bible meaning of death.

Just recently I came upon a poem by E. F. McNamara which pictures the slow but certain death of the sinner. It pictures the hypocrite as he goes down in sin:

> He knew the terrible effects of sin,
> And waited for deterioration's slow
> But ruthless change. He waited for the flow
> Of evil to surcharge his veins, begin
> To show up through his fair and youthful skin,
> And thus expose him so that all should know
> His charm was but a mist which did not show
> The filth and rottenness which lay within.

He waited. But his youth defied the change
So well, a ghostly hope flew through his mind.
(Perhaps he would escape, perhaps some strange
Miscarriage of his fate would use him kind.)
But now, not even blest with slow decay,
He knows he'll crumble shockingly one day.

—*Spirit.*

The second truth that shines out in the statement, "dying, thou shalt die," is that the end of dying spiritually is eternal death. You have heard the story of Faust. It is one of the greatest stories of all time because it deals in a masterful way with one of the great realities of human nature and of the spiritual world. Satan and Doctor Faust made a bargain. They both agreed that there are two worlds—this present world and the world to come. Satan agreed to bind himself to "run and never rest" at the call of Faust here in this life, if Faust would do as much for him in the world to come. Faust agreed, and began his life of partnership with Satan. *Faust began to go down,*—always going from bad to worse. Finally, when his bad life, which was a living death, was at an end, he realized that his day of doom was at hand, and one hour before midnight, his time to die, Faust soliloquized:

Ah Faustus,
Now hast thou but one bare hour to live!
And then thou must be damned perpetually!
Stand still, ye ever moving spheres of heaven,
That time may cease, and midnight never come.
Fair Nature's eye, rise, rise again, and make
Perpetual day; or let this hour be but
A year, a month, a week, a natural day,
That Faustus may repent and save his soul!

O slowly, slowly run, ye steeds of night!
The stars move still, time runs, the clock will strike,
The devil will come, and Faustus must be
Forever damned!

"Dying, thou shalt die!" All of a man's life in sin is but a living death; and the end of this living death is eternal death! When death overtakes a man who is dead in sin, he passes out into a place where he is "forever damned." That is the wages for a life-time of service to Satan.

Faustus was in sight of his "pay in full" before his soul left the body! And, my sinner friends, the story of Faustus illustrates just how it will be with every soul that has sold out to Satan. He tells you that he will do many wonderful things for you while you are in this world, if you will just serve him and do his bidding. Are you willing to make such a bargain? You will feel the horrors of eternal damnation just as Faustus felt them, if you continue your bargain with Satan. Why not ask God to help and save you now? I plead with you not to wait till your dying hour. You will pray then, but your prayer may be too late. Do not make the mistake Faustus made!

A few summers ago I was holding a revival meeting in a village in eastern North Carolina, near the Dismal Swamp. I was rooming in the village hotel. I never felt hotter weather than we had there during those days, neither have I ever seen more mosquitoes and candleflies than I saw there. The only lights in the little hotel were carbide gas lights, the hottest flame ever installed in a house for lighting purposes! They did not even have screens in the windows to keep the flies and mosquitoes out.

At night, after services, I would go up and light the lamps long enough to see where things were located, and to get settled for the night. I shall never forget one thing, however, that happened in that little hot room almost every night. As soon as I turned on those lights little white moths would swarm through the windows, and dash themselves like snowflakes into the white heat of those gas jets! Into the gas flames they dashed themselves, and then—what was left of them—those little waifs of the night would spiral to the floor, like fairy flying machines falling to the earth and to death!

As I saw those wee things dashing themselves into the flames, and to sure and hopeless death, I could but think how silly it was for them to do it! I felt sorry for them. I felt that their instincts should have kept them from destroying themselves that way. But then I thought of the millions of human beings who are living in sin, and I said to myself, "They are just as foolish as those little moths! and a million times more foolish!" The moths didn't really know any better; and it didn't matter much about them anyway. But for a human being to destroy himself—it is a tragedy for two worlds—for time and eternity!

IV

Now, my unsaved friends, I want you to be saved. "For the wages of sin is death; but the gift of God is eternal life through Jesus Christ our Lord."

I want you to accept God's gift, which is eternal life. Sin undermines character, it destroys peace, it is always at war with the love of God, it blackens and stains the whole life, it blights and kills! . . . "But the gift of God is eternal life."

The way to freedom, to life, and to peace is open to you. You do not have to serve sin and draw the wages of eternal death. You are a free moral agent; you can change masters. You can choose Christ as your Master; and the moment you make that choice, you become the recipient of God's great gift, which is the good, happy, abundant, and eternal life! It is the life that is satisfying for this world, and for the hour of death, and for vast eternity!

And, my sinner friends, you can have this life—you can have it now and forever—if you will only break with Satan and take Christ as your Saviour and Lord! Take him—open your heart—be done with sin—be done with death—lay hold on eternal life—be saved tonight!

V

ARE YOU SELLING YOUR SOUL?

For what shall it profit a man, if he shall gain the whole world, and lose his own soul? or what shall a man give in exchange for his soul?—MARK 8: 36, 37.

The question I am asking you tonight is suggested by this text, and it is this: "Are You Selling Your Soul?" Every day we see all sorts of advertisements of wares for sale. The papers are full of them; the radio sings and barks them; the show-windows of the stores are bursting with them; our streets and highways are cluttered with them.

But did it ever occur to you that millions of people are selling their souls? Did it ever occur to you that all about you there are people who, if they were labeled according to their spiritual condition and attitude, would be wearing across their breasts placards bearing the legend, "My Soul for Sale"? There are millions of people who have their souls on the market; and our text is God's solemn question to them—"For what shall it profit a man, if he shall gain the whole world, and lose his own soul? or what shall a man give in exchange for his soul?"

I bring this text to you tonight, and ask you to think with me about it.

I

First, this text suggests that the soul is the most valuable object in the universe. Just recently the United States Government let the contract for two "impregnable vaults" for the nation's nine-billion-dollar stock

[73]

of gold. These vaults are to be built in the safest spots in the United States, and made as nearly impregnable as modern science can make them. They are to protect the nation's gold.

I also read recently an article which said that the bed of the ocean in some places is strewn with the wrecks of ships, and that several great companies were being organized to put new deep-sea-diving methods into use to recover the treasures from some of the great ships that were sunk during the World War.

I think it is wise for the United States to safeguard its gold; and it is all right for men to put modern science to work to recover sunken treasures from the bed of the ocean. But I am thinking tonight of a treasure far greater than all the gold in the world, and infinitely more precious than any jewel that ever went down on a sinking ship! I am thinking about lost souls. Your souls, my friends, are the most valuable objects in the universe. Jesus, when he asked the question of our text, clearly implied that he considered one soul of infinitely more value than "the whole world."

You recall the second temptation of Jesus. Satan took him up on a high mountain and showed him all the kingdoms of this world, and the glory of them, and then said to him, "All these things will I give thee, if thou wilt fall down and worship me." But what did Jesus do? Jesus knew that if the devil could actually deliver the goods on his proposal, it would be a bad bargain for him to sell his soul to Satan for the whole world.

Not only did Jesus refuse to sell himself to Satan, but he taught incessantly that the soul should be given first place in all man's thinking. He said that the kingdom of God was like a man seeking goodly pearls, "who, when he had found one pearl of great price, went and sold all that he had, and bought it." Jesus taught the supreme value of the soul when he said, "If thy right eye offend thee, pluck it out," and when he said, "If thy right hand offend thee, cut it off." Nothing is dearer to a man than his right eye, or his right hand; yet Jesus emphatically declared that it was better for a man to enter into life maimed than for his whole body to perish. Jesus was trying to impress his hearers that the salvation of the soul was the supreme concern of man. He had better suffer the loss of anything, or all things, rather than the loss of his soul. The soul is that divine element in man that makes him like God, that enables him to think God's thoughts after him, and which is as immortal as God himself.

God sets the soul of man above every other object in the universe in value; the soul of man is God's supreme concern of all creation. So far as we know, or can imagine, under the present condition of things, in the vast universe there is no other spark of life outside our world! God has here in the life of his people—the souls of men—a treasure so far surpassing all other objects that there can be no comparison! This is why God sets such store by every immortal soul. We are verily God's offspring, and he loves us with an everlasting love.

II. Second, this text suggests that, notwithstanding the fact that the soul is the most valuable object in the universe, some people sell their souls. We know some people who are selling their souls. What are they selling them for? What do they get for them? What are they asking in exchange for them?

Now, as I see it, people are selling their souls for two things—just two things: they are selling them for *money,* and for *sinful pleasure.*

People are selling their souls for *money*—material things—property, houses, lands, banks, stores, stocks, bonds, and the like. It is a sad, solemn fact that most men value material things more highly than they do spiritual things, temporal things more highly than they do eternal things. The Bible abounds with examples of men who sold their souls for material things, simply because they gave material things first place in their lives, when they should have put spiritual things first.

The rich farmer that Jesus told about sold his soul for material gain. He was prosperous, his land brought forth bountifully, he was making more stuff than he could store. He said to himself: "What shall I do? . . . I know what I will do; I will tear down my old barns and I will build me greater ones, and there will I store all my goods, and when I have all my barns full, I will say to my soul, 'Soul, thou hast much goods laid up for many years; take thine ease, eat, drink, and be merry.'" But just then God said to him, "Thou fool, this night is thy soul required of thee: then whose shall those things be, which thou hast provided?" That man was selling his soul because he was putting business success first in his life, and cared nothing about being "rich towards God."

You know the story of Dives. That rich man had every comfort of life; he lived in a mansion, was clothed in purple and fine linen, and fared sumptuously every day. He was totally unconcerned about the welfare of his fellow man. He was perfectly willing to let all the rest of the world starve to death at his very door, without so much as lifting his little finger to help them! You recall that he let poor Lazarus, sick and suffering, lie at his very front gate and die of exposure and starvation. That rich man had sold his soul for the luxurious comfort of this material world. He cared nothing for his soul while he lived; but when he died and lifted up his eyes in Hades with all its torments, he realized that he had made the most awful mistake that a man ever made in the world!

At the close of the World War, the richest man in Germany was Hugo Stinnes. The German *Who's Who,* issued before the war began, gave a long list of his industrial triumphs. The war developed his genius for organization. His millions multiplied. After the war, when others were impoverished, his abundant capital overseas and his worldwide credit gave him a lead over all his rivals. As his nation sank, he mounted. When others wept for the ruined fatherland, he brazenly told the interviewers, "I own Germany." His name was familiar in every land. He was the world's richest man!

At the age of fifty-four his health failed. He went to the hospital for an operation. It didn't turn out well. Two other operations were performed, and then it was announced to the world that Hugo Stinnes had pneumonia and was not expected to live. As the hour of death drew near for him, a correspondent, watching at the hospital, wrote this dispatch:

"The reporters are smoking cigarettes on the hospital steps, while they wait for him to die. On the exchanges the speculators are ready to profit from the sharp declines that are expected in the stock of his many corporations the moment he expires. But in the sick room, where he must be slowly losing grip on his nerves, is it possible that he recalls his most famous boast, 'Frankly, I worship on the altar of Big Business'?"

No more conspicuous example of selling the soul for mammon exists in the records of mankind! But what did it profit him? Exactly nothing!

People are also selling their souls for *sinful pleasure*. I suspect there are some here tonight who have persistently refused to accept Christ as their Saviour because they have some sin in their lives which they are not willing to give up. You find pleasure in sin, and because you find pleasure in sin you will sell your souls for it.

Esau sold his birthright for a mess of pottage, and thousands of young people are selling their souls for a few days, or years, of sinful pleasure. The sinful pleasure of many in our day is drinking whiskey. Young people know that drunkenness is a ruinous habit; they know that whiskey is habit-forming and the enemy of everything good in the world. Yet, because it dethrones the reason, and gives a feeling of greatness and exaltation, people are not only selling their souls for it, but are trying to make the world believe that it is smart to drink!

Now I want to read to you a few verses from God's Word about this sinful pleasure. First of all, I want to read to you the sternest law ever written, so far as I know, about drunkenness. It is found in Deuteronomy

21: 18-21. Here it is: "If a man have a stubborn and rebellious son, which will not obey the voice of his father, or the voice of his mother, and that, when they have chastened him, will not hearken unto them: then shall his father and his mother lay hold on him, and bring him out unto the elders of his city, and unto the gate of his place; and they shall say unto the elders of his city, This our son is stubborn and rebellious, he will not obey our voice; he is a glutton, and a drunkard." Here you see a son who is stubborn and rebellious, and who ends up with being a glutton and a drunkard. Now what did that old law say should be done with such a boy? Here is what it says: "And all the men of his city shall stone him with stones, that he die: so shalt thou put evil away from among you; and all Israel shall hear, and fear." That was the old Mosaic law. It was a stern law, but it shows how God's people of the long ago felt on the question of a stubborn, rebellious, gluttonous and drunken child!

Let me read to you another passage from the Bible, this time from the New Testament. It is found in First Corinthians 5: 11, "But now I have written unto you not to keep company, if any man that is called a brother be a fornicator, or covetous, or an idolater, or a railer, or a drunkard, or an extortioner; with such an one no not to eat." In this passage we have a horrible list of sinners, all of whom are selling their souls for what they count as sinful pleasure, and the drunkard is placed right along with the fornicator, the idolater, the extortioner, and the rest.

Let me read you two more verses from the same book, the sixth chapter and the ninth and tenth verses:

"Know ye not that the unrighteous shall not inherit the kingdom of God? Be not deceived: neither fornicators, nor idolaters, nor adulterers, nor effeminate, nor abusers of themselves with mankind, nor thieves, nor covetous, nor drunkards, nor revilers, nor extortioners, shall inherit the kingdom of God." Here we have the plain Word of God about the drunkard and many other sinners. They are all right along together, a bad company of sinners—idolaters, adulterers, thieves, and abusers of themselves with mankind—and all of them are plainly warned that they shall not "inherit the kingdom of God."

Yet everywhere we turn liquor-lovers are trying to make liquor-drinking respectable. I want to ask you if anything that shuts the door of the kingdom of God in a man's face can be made respectable? According to the passage I have just read, drunkenness is just as respectable in the sight of God as being a thief! It is just as respectable as being an adulterer! It is just as respectable as being an idolater! Yet men are selling their souls for these sins and for the pleasure they find in them!

Yes, people are selling their souls for sinful pleasure, and for the hope of material gain; and when they have made the bargain and closed the deal, they have lost everything in the universe worth having—they have lost holiness, which is their passport to happiness for this world and for the world to come—and along with the loss of holiness, they have lost hope, for there is no buying back the soul when once this fateful bargain has been closed in death!

III

Now I want to show you, if I can, the utter folly of selling your soul for these things!

First, think of the folly of selling your soul for *earthly gain*—for money and for the things money can buy! Think again of Dives who sold his soul for earthly wealth and for sinful ease. He had everything that his heart desired so far as this world was concerned. He had it all, while folks were starving at his door. He enjoyed it until he died, then he woke up in Hades and lifted up his eyes, being in torment. Then he would have given his whole fortune for a few drops of water to cool his tongue. Sinner friends—you money-loving men, you worldlings who think only of material things —do you think that Dives was wise in selling his soul for the sake of a big house, for the sake of ease and luxury for a few years here on the earth, and then dying and leaving everything to folks who were probably glad the day he died? Do you think he was wise, going out to spend eternity in torment because of his life of self-ishness here? Do you think he was wise? No; you know he wasn't; you know he was a fool!

Think of that prosperous farmer I spoke of a little while ago. He sold his soul for the sake of getting rich. He shut up his heart against the needs of his fellows; he worked hard to lay up much goods for many years. He planned to take his ease, and was going to have a good time "after a while." But you recall that suddenly, when he was least expecting it, God said to him, "Thou fool, this night thy soul is required of thee." He was snatched away from all his wealth, and could not take one penny of it with him. He had left

God out. Do you think he was wise? Of course you don't; you know he was a fool! God's Word says that he was a fool!

Sometime ago I heard a story of two brothers which greatly impressed me. They were hard workers, and devoted to each other. They hardly took time to eat, or sleep. From early morning till late at night they raced at their work. They ran a mill, a cotton gin, a garage, a store, and several farms. They never had time to go to church, nor to think of religion, nor to think of their souls. Unexpectedly one of them took pneumonia and died. For the first time in his life the surviving brother was shocked into a consciousness of the uncertainty of life, and the certainty of death. In the wee hours of the night he went over to their store to get some clothes in which to bury his brother. As he gathered up the few articles in which his brother was to be buried, and laid them on the counter, he thought to himself, "This is pitiful! John worked himself to death trying to get rich! And now before he was forty years old he is gone, and all that will ever be of any use to him is that little pile of clothes!" He told these thoughts afterwards. But all men who are living only for the accumulation of material things, and are not concerned about their souls, are doing just what that fine young man did!

Think also of the folly of selling your soul for *sinful pleasure!* I want to say four things about sinful pleasure which will show you, I think, the utter folly of selling your soul for it.

First, the pleasures of sin are *short-lived.* You recall that Moses was brought up in the house of Pharaoh, surrounded with all the pleasure of a king's palace. But the Bible tells us that when he came to years of maturity he made the best choice that he ever made in his life. God was calling him; God had a great work for him to do; God wanted him to lead the Children of Israel out of Egyptian bondage. On the other hand, he could have remained in the palace of the king, and could have counted himself the son of Pharaoh's daughter. But the Bible tells us that "By faith Moses . . . refused to be called the son of Pharaoh's daughter; choosing rather to suffer affliction with the people of God, than to enjoy the pleasures of sin for a season." Moses saw that the pleasures of sin were but "for a season." He knew that the pleasures of sin are short-lived, and that, therefore, it is foolish for a man to sell his soul for them.

Again, the pleasures of sin are not only short-lived, but they invariably leave a *sting—a burning, deadly sting*. Whoever sins, suffers. It is a law of God and nature. Adam and Eve were driven from the Garden of Eden because of their sin. That is a symbol of the sting of sin!

If ever in all the world two people proved by their own experience the folly of selling their souls for sinful pleasures, it was Antony and Cleopatra. Theirs was an illicit love affair, as everyone knows. Cleopatra was one of the most bewitching of all women, and Antony one of the greatest of all rulers. They gave way to sin, and launched upon what they fancied would be a sea of pleasure. But they soon found that sin drowns men in destruction. After a brief season of sinful pleasure, both Antony and Cleopatra died the death of suicides, and, as if it were a symbol of her folly, the very asp that stung the life out of Cleopatra was brought to her in a basket of figs and flowers! The pleasures of sin are the figs and flowers of a day! They always end in death!

The third thing I wish to say about the pleasures of sin is that they *diminish the more one sins!* Sin is like a habit-forming drug, and sinful pleasure is like the effect of such a drug—the dose must continually be increased to produce the desired effect. The end of such folly is death.

The fourth and last thing I want to say about sinful pleasure is that *it is expensive.* Sin robs of everything in life that is worth having. Samson was the slave to sin, and he is a picture of every man who is selling his soul for sinful pleasure. His sins first unmanned him; then they weakened his will, and destroyed his power to resist his enemies; then they bound him; then they blinded him; then they put him to grinding at the mill of his enemies; and finally they utterly destroyed him. He paid a dear price for his sinful pleasure. Oh, the folly of it!

Thomas W. Faber, in a few poignant lines, expressed the truth about sin. These lines were found a few years ago written on a crumpled piece of paper clutched in the dead hand of a young woman who had fallen into sin, and who in desperation had committed suicide:

> There is not one evil that sin has not brought me.
>
> There is not one good that has come in its train.
>
> It has cursed me through life, and its sorrows have sought me

Each day that went by, in want, sickness, or pain.
And when this life of affliction is ended,
What a home for my weary heart has it prepared!
And the night, the sick night of eternal despair.

The pleasures of sin are always uncertain; the punishment of sin is inevitable: the gain of sin is purely fanciful and temporary; the loss of sin is positive and eternal!

IV

Now, in the light of all that I have said, I come back to my text, and ask you again, "What shall it profit a man, if he shall gain the whole world, and lose his own soul? or what shall a man give in exchange for his soul?" We can make the case no stronger than this text. It is God's question to everyone here tonight. I want you to be saved; I want you to give your soul into the keeping of Christ. Paul said, "I know whom I have believed, and am persuaded that he is able to keep that which I have committed unto him against that day." My friends, I know Christ Jesus will forgive your sins, and will keep your soul secure forever if you will commit your life to him. I plead with you tonight not to sell your soul to Satan.

About a hundred years ago the famous Methodist preacher, Rowland Hill, of England, was preaching in a London park. Lady Ann Erskine, as well known in her day as Lady Astor is known in ours, chanced to be driving by, and inquired who the preacher was. Upon being told that he was Rowland Hill, the unique Methodist preacher, she desired to see him, and therefore directed her coachman to drive up close to the platform upon which the preacher was standing. Instantly Hill recognized her, and it chanced that he was preaching on the very text that I am using: "What shall it profit a man, if he shall gain the whole world, and lose his own soul? or what shall a man give in exchange for his soul?" Pausing for an instant when Lady Erskine drove up, he began in a different tone: "I have something to sell; I have more than a little to sell; I have more than a crown of Europe to sell—it's the soul of Lady Ann Erskine! Is there anyone who bids for it? Yes, I hear a bid—Satan is bidding! Satan, what will you give? What will you give? 'I will give pleasure, honor, riches; yes, I will give the whole world for her soul.' Is there anyone else who bids? Do I hear another bid?—Yes, the Lord Jesus Christ bids! He says: 'I will give you peace, joy, comfort that the world knows not of. Yes, I will give eternal life.' Lady Ann Erskine, you have heard the two bids for your soul. Which will you take?" There and then she opened the door of her carriage and came forward weeping, and accepted the Lord Jesus Christ as her Saviour!

May God help you tonight to be as wise as was Lady Ann Erskine. May you not sell your soul to Satan, but may you come now to Christ and be saved. Again I ask you: "What shall it profit a man, if he shall gain the whole world, and lose his own soul? or what will a man give in exchange for his soul?" Will you not answer this question now by surrendering your life and soul to Christ?

VI

WHAT MUST WE DO TO BE SAVED?

What must I do to be saved?—ACTS 16: 30.

Someone has said that this is the soul's greatest question. I am inclined to think that it is. There are many great questions, however, such as, "Where shall I spend eternity?" or, "Is there a future life?" or, "What shall I do with Jesus?" or, "How shall we escape if we neglect so great salvation?" All these are great questions, but they are all comprehended in the question of our text, "What must I do to be saved?"

Paul and Silas had heard the Macedonian call, "Come over into Macedonia, and help us." In response to that call they had come to Philippi, the chief city of Macedonia, and on the Sabbath day had gone out of the city by the riverside to a prayer meeting. And there was a woman there by the name of Lydia whose heart God opened to accept Jesus Christ as her Saviour, and she was baptized that very hour; and after her conversion she became a helper of the gospel. She besought Paul and Silas to make her home headquarters while they were in that community.

Now, there was in Philippi a strange sort of young woman who had "a spirit of divination." She was a sort of fortune-teller, who made a great deal of money for her managers. For many days as Paul and Silas made their way out to the place of prayer, that young woman followed them, crying out, "These men are the servants of the most high God, which shew unto us the way of salvation." She kept that up for a long time,

[87]

until finally Paul, being annoyed by it, turned and said to the spirit in her, "I command thee in the name of Jesus Christ to come out of her." And immediately the spirit came out of her.

When her masters saw that their hope of profits was gone, they seized Paul and Silas and dragged them into court and accused them of breaking the law, and making a great disturbance in town. The crowd also joined in the attack upon them, and as a result the officers had them beaten and thrown in jail. That night, however, Paul and Silas were praying and singing hymns, and the other prisoners were listening. Suddenly there was such an earthquake that the jail was shaken to its foundations; all the doors flew open, and the chains of the prisoners were unfastened. It woke the jailer, and when he saw the doors all open, and imagined that the prisoners were all out and gone, he drew his sword and was about to kill himself. Paul called to him and told him not to harm himself, that the prisoners were all there. Then the jailer got a light and rushed in, and fell trembling at the feet of Paul and Silas, and asked the question of our text, "What must I do to be saved?"

Paul answered that question by saying, "Believe on the Lord Jesus Christ, and thou shalt be saved, and thy house." And he and all his family believed and were saved, and were baptized by Paul and Silas that hour. What a victory for Christ! and what a victory for the jailer and his household! I would to God that every unsaved person in this congregation tonight might be saved as suddenly and wonderfully as was that Philippian jailer! Let us, therefore, examine this question, "What must I do to be saved?"

I

"What must I do to be saved?" First, let us disabuse our minds of some of the inadequate and misleading theories of men as to how we are saved.

The first of these erroneous theories that I mention is the theory that God from the foundation of the world chose certain men and angels to enjoy salvation and felicity, while he left all others to reprobation, to helpless rejection and damnation.

There was a time when this fatalistic doctrine lay like a pall over the spirits of men. People waited for God as if they were dead men, only mumbling that if God wanted them saved he would save them, and that it was no concern of theirs. They spent all their religious energies trying to resolve the problem of the human will—as to whether we are bound or free.

We know that Paul plants and Apollos waters, and that God gives the increase. We know that in raising a crop man plows the ground, plants the seed and cultivates the growing plant; but God gives the increase. We can do nothing apart from God, and it is God that worketh in us both to will and to do; and apart from this first motion on God's part we will never desire to live according to the will of God. But God desires that all men should be saved, and has made ample provision for the salvation of men and women through repentance and faith in Jesus Christ. Even John Calvin was not the stern fatalist that he has been represented as being. In his comment on 1 John 2:2, "He is the propitiation for our sins: and not for our sins only, but also for the sins of the whole world"—Calvin said:

"Christ suffered for the sins of the whole world, and, in the goodness of God, salvation is offered unto all men without distinction, his blood being shed not for a part of the world only, but for the whole race; for although in the world nothing is found worthy of the favor of God, yet he holds out the propitiation of the whole world, since without exception he summons all to the faith of Christ, which is nothing else than the door of hope." This is what I say to you, sinner friends: God summons you now to faith in Christ; the offer of salvation is sincerely made to you, and whosoever will believe, to them he gives the power to become the children of God.

But we must remember, as Alexander Maclaren says, that "notwithstanding the universality of the Divine loving-kindness, mankind still parts into two sections, one capable of receiving the highest gifts, one incapable, because not desiring them. Therefore, the One Light, in its universal shining, works two effects, being luster and life to such as welcome it, but darkness and death to those who turn from it. It is man's awful prerogative that he can distil poison out of the water of life, and can make it impossible for himself to receive from tender, universal Goodness anything but destruction." We must remember that God does not force our wills. He offers us salvation and urges us to accept it. But your salvation depends upon your own desire: if you want to be saved, there is salvation for you: God has made provision for you: the door of hope is open for you. It is your choice, however, to come in, or to stay out. There is no man in all the world who is left uninvited. Any doctrine to the contrary is erroneous.

A second error as to how men are saved is the belief that certain rites performed in the name of religion are effective in securing the regeneration of the soul, the forgiveness of sin, and the admission of the individual into the company of the redeemed. This error was widely held in the past, and is quite common today.

This error of thinking that external rites can effect salvation takes various forms, such as pilgrimages to sacred shrines like Mecca, Benares, and Rome; or certain lustral acts, such as the blood bath of the Orphic mysteries, the washing of the multitudes in the waters of the Ganges, or the rite of baptism as practiced in some of our Christian churches; or the participation in a ritual meal, after the fashion of the initiates in the cult of Mithra, the mystic meal of Iranian votaries, or the Holy communion as observed in some Christian groups; or the observance of circumcision by the Jews, the use of a prayer-wheel as among the Tibitans, or the repetition of prescribed formulas, like the "On mani padmi hum" of the Buddhists, the "Bismillah" of the Moslems, or the "Ave Marias" and "Pater Nosters" of the Roman Catholics. We know, however, there is no outward work, or act, that can save the soul from death! Christ spent most of his time during his public ministry trying to disabuse the minds of men of the error that rites of any sort could make the soul right. Salvation is not to be had in any such fashion.

Neither is salvation to be attained by membership in any organization, no matter how valuable such an organization may be. The church has sometimes been thought of as an "ark of safety" for those who wished to escape the damnation of hell. People were taught to

believe that the church had power to save. Even infants
were taken into the church because the priests taught
that the church was a saving institution, or that the
ordinances of the church were saving rites. But it
should be understood clearly that membership in a
church does not save; it does not regenerate the soul, nor
procure the forgiveness of sin. One might have his
name on all the church rolls in Christendom without
being saved.

Neither is the acceptance of a creed, nor the stout de-
fense of any formulation of religious doctrine of any
effect in the salvation of the soul from death. Salvation
comes from a different quarter; salvation comes from
union with Christ, and that union does not depend upon
the acceptance of a creedal statement about Christ.
Union with Christ is far deeper, higher, broader, and
more fundamental than the outward acceptance of a
creed. One may utter all the creedal statements in the
world with his lips while his heart is filled with unholiness.

II

Secondly, let us ask, "What is meant by being
saved?" When the Philippian jailer cried out, "Sirs,
what must I do to be saved?" what did he mean? What
do we mean when we say that a person is saved?

Many of us have inadequate notions as to what salvation is, and in order that we may get a clearer conception of the meaning of salvation, let us turn to the
New Testament and see what it says about the matter.
In many instances in the New Testament, salvation
relates to deliverance from disease, or from demoniacal
possession. In many instances it relates to the rescue

of the physical life from impending peril, or from instant death; while in many other instances it relates to spiritual deliverance from the power and guilt of sin. All these passages are based upon the thought that salvation is deliverance from that which is undesirable and bad, to that which is desirable and good. Jesus said that he came to seek and to save that which was lost and to give his life a ransom for many; that he came that the world through him might be saved. He came that men might have abundant life—a better and more abounding life than they could ever have apart from him.

Now what is the essence of this salvation?

First, it involves the forgiveness of sin. No soul that clings to sin can claim to be saved. Our sins have separated us from God, and have plunged us into despair.

Second, salvation means justification—that is, the remission of all punishment due to the sinner and the restoration of the soul to God's favor and fellowship. But God cannot justify an ungodly man apart from his faith in Christ; but on the basis of the sinner's faith in Christ, God does forgive the sinner, and declare him acquitted before God; this is the full and complete pardon of the sinner before the court of God's eternal justice. It is an act of God, whereby he declares the sinner now fully absolved, just as a father, personally injured and grieved by the sin of his child, shows mercy and forgiveness to his own child when he repents and asks for mercy and restoration on the basis of repentance and faith. When God gives us the status in his presence of a righteous person, it is because we are right in our hearts; it is because we, like the prodigal, have seen our mistakes and have come back to our Father, and have pledged ourselves to do his will in the future.

But salvation means more than the forgiveness of sin and the restoration to God's fellowship; it means deliverance from the *power* of sin, from the *dominion* of sin; it is the *breaking* of the "law of sin" in our hearts. It is the impartation of a new principle of life. Salvation literally means the entrance of the eternal Spirit into our hearts in such a way that the Spirit that was in Christ actually becomes our life principle, and Christ becomes our Master, so that his work of grace in our hearts begins operating to bring us more and more into his own likeness, and to enable us more and more to die unto sin and to live unto righteousness. This great spiritual change we call regeneration.

And, finally, salvation means deliverance from evil, such as the fears and anxieties of life, and the dread of death; and it is the ridding of one's life of all unholy conduct and dispositions, and the filling of the heart and mind with love and peace and joy by the Holy Spirit which dwells within us. This is what is meant by salvation. It is the new life in Christ.

III

How may we obtain this salvation? What must we do to be saved? How do we actually *appropriate* this salvation for ourselves?

In the beginning of this message I told you how salvation is *not* to be had; now I want to tell you how salvation *can* be had.

You can be saved in exactly the same way that the Philippian jailer was saved. We come back and center our attention upon him. He is a striking example of a sinner getting saved, and if he could get saved there is hope for you to get saved, even before this service is ended.

As we look at that man, we see that he had an earnest desire to be saved. He saw himself a sinner, and then he came and fell at the feet of Paul and Silas and cried out: "What must I do to be saved?" He was interested; he was in earnest; he wanted to be saved; and, as I told you a little while ago, God wants you to be saved; he has made ample provision for your salvation. But God cannot save you unless you desire to be saved. God uses all the means at his command to get you to want to be saved. He uses the truth that I am preaching to you; he uses all the warnings of the Bible to head you off from going to destruction; he uses all the promises of his blessings for this world and for the world to come to get you to look up and seek the best; he shows you his love for you, and commends his love to you by the gift of Jesus Christ to die in your behalf; he wants you to love him! God so loved the world that he gave his only begotten Son, to come into the world to die for you to show you how much he loved you! Now if the death of Christ will not win the love of lost men and women to God, then there is nothing else that God can do to win their love. They are hopelessly bound to sin, and there is nothing else that God can do to save them. So, the first step in getting saved is to want to be saved. If you have no feeling about the matter, if you have no desire to be right in God's sight, if you have no interest in your own salvation, you are of all men most pitiable. You may be beyond the reach of grace. The only thing that God can do for you is to offer you salvation, and if you do not want it, then you are hopeless, unless a miracle of grace quickens you and stirs your heart to seek after God. I pray God that you may see your need and that you may feel your need of salvation tonight!

In the second place, when the Philippian jailer came and fell down before Paul and Silas and asked, "What must I do to be saved?" Paul told him to do one thing—just one thing—"Believe on the Lord Jesus Christ, and thou shalt be saved." Paul did not split the kindling too fine, as the good country people used to say about a certain type of preaching; neither did he put the fodder too high. He said it all in one word—"Believe." But there are many anxious souls, who do not understand just what we mean by "believing on the Lord Jesus Christ." I want to make this so plain that any boy or girl here who feels distressed because of sin, and wants to be right with God, may understand how to exercise saving faith. Dr. Austin Crouch, in his little book, *The Plan of Salvation,* has well said that you might take two men, one of them saved and the other lost, and put them in a dungeon with walls a mile thick, and chain them there, flat on their backs, and go out and close up the hole behind you, leaving them there in midnight darkness, and there would not be anything necessary for the salvation of that lost man that the saved man could not tell him, and that the lost man could not do, lying there flat on his back. All that he would have to do would be to believe on the Lord Jesus Christ!

But what does believing on Christ mean?

It means, first of all, that you realize you are a sinner; that you know you are wrong in God's sight, and that you need salvation. That is the first step towards believing.

It means, too, that you desire to be done with sin. As I have already said, there is no hope of salvation for anyone who does not want to be saved. And no matter what else may happen to a lost soul, salvation is impossible so long as that soul is unconcerned about salvation. So I urge you, sinner friends, to own your sins; do not deny them, nor blame them on someone else. I pray that you may see how hateful sin is in God's sight. There is no hope for you to be saved until you realize that your sins have separated you from God, and that your sins are hateful in his sight.

The next step is to realize that Christ is your Saviour, your only hope of salvation! He came to seek and to save that which was lost. Whatever was needed for your full restoration to God's loving favor, Christ has accomplished; he has made complete and full provision for your return to God. All the benefits of his redeeming work come to you by simply taking Christ as your Saviour, and saying, "From this time till death I will follow thee." The moment you say that from your heart and step out and confess him as your Saviour and Lord, there and then God forgives all your past sins, and writes your name down in the Lamb's book of life, and you are God's child, fully and freely forgiven, and reinstated in God's household, no matter what your sins of the past have been!

The prodigal, out in the far country of sin, in rags and filth, hungry, friendless, dejected, and homesick, is a picture of the sinner away from God, but with hope. When he came to himself, and resolved to get up out of his sin, and go back to his father, he was like a sinner turning with sorrow from his sins. He saw what sin was doing for him. Instead of finding pleasure in sin, as he had been persuaded that he would, he found nothing but sorrow and disappointment. He saw that sin was stripping him of everything in the world that was worth having, and leaving only ruin in its place. Then he resolved to get up and go back to his father, and confess his sin and ask forgiveness. His heart was broken because of his sin, and it was broken from his sin. Whenever a sinner comes to the place that he is willing to do as that prodigal did, the worst of his struggle is over: he is not far from the kingdom: he is almost saved. He has the three C's which spell true repentance —conviction, contrition, and conversion—which mean turning from the far country of sin and facing about towards home. The prodigal had all this to his credit when he started back to his father's house.

But before the prodigal found peace he had to do more than repent; he had to go to his father and confess his sin, and throw himself upon his father's mercy. That is what the sinner must do before he can find peace. That was what Paul told the jailer to do. When he told him to believe on the Lord Jesus Christ, he meant that he should commit himself unreservedly to the mercy and goodness of Christ, and to trust him for pardon. That is what believing in Christ means. Paul knew that if the jailer would stake his soul's salvation on Christ, he would find forgiveness and peace. He knew that he would find rest for his soul, and that his heart would be filled with such a sense of peace and forgiveness that he would know that he was accepted of God.

I urge you, therefore, sinner friends, to come back home tonight! He will welcome you back. If you were bitten by a deadly serpent, and the doctor should come and offer you an antidote that would certainly save your life, you would not hesitate and question. You would take the saving remedy. If you held it in your hand, however, and argued about it, or questioned its efficacy, and refused to take it, you would but perish. If you had confidence in the doctor you would take the remedy at once.

Christ is the only remedy for your salvation. You can be saved if you will only commit yourself to him, with faith that he is the Saviour. If you will try this remedy, you will find that it works: you will find that he does give peace and forgiveness. You will find that when you walk with him, he will lead you into fellowship with God, so that you will feel the presence of God in your very heart, and such a peace as you have never felt since you first realized that you were a sinner! To believe in Christ, to have faith in Christ, is to lay aside your own philosophies, your own ways of trying to find salvation, and to adopt the way of life that Christ exemplified and taught; and it is a fact that if we do this, the very life of God will come into our hearts and fill us with a sense of forgiveness and peace, with a sense of wholeness and integration with the Universe, so that the soul "hitherto divided and consciously wrong, inferior, and unhappy, becomes unified and consciously right, superior, and happy." My sinner friends, do not stay to question; come and put Christ to the test!

You do not have to understand *how* this can be. All you need to do is to commit yourself to Christ, and begin living according to his will. You do not have to know how food nourishes your body before you can eat and grow; you do not have to know how medicine acts to save your life before it will do its work, if it is taken. When Christ was talking to Nicodemus in the third chapter of John, he tried to explain to him "how" a soul is born again. He told him that he need not bother about *how* it could be; he simply told him that it was like any other mystery. Nobody can tell how God creates our physical bodies; just so, nobody can explain just how we are born of the Spirit. But Jesus illustrated it by likening it to the blowing of the wind. Nobody can tell whence the wind cometh, nor whither it goeth; but anybody can tell when the wind is blowing. So it is with everyone that is born of the Spirit; we can know by experience when we are born of the Spirit.

Some years ago I went through the Mammoth Cave. But I never could have made that trip without a guide; without a guide I would have been hopelessly lost. But my guide knew all about the cave, and knew the path perfectly; he knew all the ups and downs and crooks and turns, and all the beautiful places, and all the dangerous places; and with his light and his knowledge he was able to lead us in a good, safe way, and make the journey a perfect delight, and then at last to lead us out into the light of the world without. But we had to trust our guide, and we did trust him; our lives depended upon it!

That is a parable of how Christ saves us. Life is like going through the Mammoth Cave just one time; and to make this journey of life we need a guide; we must have a guide, or we are hopelessly lost! Now Christ is our guide through this dark world; he knows all about life, and he knows all about the ups and downs, and the crooks and turns of this life; he knows the safe way; he knows where danger and death lurk; he knows how to lead us so that we may have the best along the way, and at last come out all right into the light of the Eternal World. But if he is to be our Guide and Saviour, we must trust him; we must believe in him; and if we believe in him, we will be saved!

My sinner friends, do you want to know what you must do to be saved? "Believe on the Lord Jesus Christ." May God help you to believe on him right now!

VII

"BE SURE YOUR SIN WILL FIND YOU OUT"

Be sure your sin will find you out.—NUMBERS 32: 23.

The Children of Israel had reached the east side of the Jordan on their way to the Promised Land. The children of Reuben and the children of Gad had a multitude of cattle; and when they saw that the land of Jazer and the land of Gilead, which had already been subjugated, was a good place for cattle, they came to Moses and Eleazer the priest and said, "If we have found grace in thy sight, let this land be given unto thy servants for a possession, and bring us not over the Jordan."

The suggestion greatly displeased Moses. He saw that Reuben and Gad were showing a yellow streak of selfishness and greed. He saw that they were trying to grab the first spoils for themselves without helping their brethren conquer the regions beyond the Jordan. He asked them, "Shall your brethren go to war, and shall ye sit here? And wherefore discourage ye the heart of the Children of Israel from going over into the land which the Lord hath given them? Thus did your fathers, when I sent them from Kadesh-barnea to see the land." Then he reminded them of the discouraging report of the ten spies, and how the Lord's anger was kindled against Israel, and how he made them to wander in the wilderness for forty years, until all that generation that had done evil in the sight of the Lord was consumed. Then they tacitly acknowledged their sin, and agreed to go over the Jordan with their brethren and help them until they obtained their inheritance, and then return to their own possessions. Moses agreed to that plan, provided they would live up to it; but he warned them that if they failed to keep their promise, "Be sure your sin will find you out."

I

Moses gives us in this text one of God's immutable laws: *Sin will find you out*.

In this world there are a great many uncertainties. Not one of us knows that he will live another year, or another month, or week. I do not know that I shall finish this sermon, or that you will live to hear it through. But we do know that our sin will find us out.

Yet Satan is always trying to fool us into thinking that we can do wrong and get away with it. My sinner friends, I plead with you to listen to the warning of this text—"Be sure your sin will find you out."

Adam and Eve in the Garden of Eden were tempted of the devil. He made light of God's commands, and told them that God did not mean what he said when he told them that if they ate of the fruit of the forbidden tree they should surely die. They listened to Satan, and disobeyed God. But no sooner had they committed sin than they were conscious of their danger and shame, and went and tried to hide themselves. But they could not hide from God, for as soon as they had hidden themselves they heard the tramp, tramp, tramp of God's feet; and then heard him calling, "Where art thou?" Ah, my sinner friends, when you do wrong, you do not have to wait long till your consciences begin to condemn you, and you begin to try to hide! But you cannot hide from God: you will hear his footsteps following you, and hear his voice calling, "Where art thou?"

Not many days ago a little mother came to see me. She was on the verge of insanity because of her remorse. She had been unfaithful to her marriage vows, even with a small baby in her arms. Her conscience was gnawing her heart out. She thought of her little girl baby and how unworthy she was to keep the child! She said, "O Preacher, my sins are killing me; I'm not fit to have my little baby; I'm afraid God will not let me keep my pracious baby! What can I do? What makes me do anything that causes me such suffering? I can't live unless I can get this burden off my heart!"

Are you trifling with sin? Are you dipping into sin here and there? I warn you from God's Book tonight —"Your sin will find you out." You will drink the bitter dregs of remorse!

Samson and Delilah played the old game of sin. They thought that they could play it without being found out. But everybody knows the strong man allowed the wiley woman to clip his locks of strength until he was bound, blinded, and put to grinding at the devil's mill of misery. There are many men in this community who are trifling with sin, as Samson did, and are flirting with death. Their sins will find them out.

A little while ago in the little town of Culpepper, Virginia, a horrible illustration of my text flared upon the public. The village undertaker, a man nearly sixty years of age, highly respected, with a lovely family of grown sons and daughters, was living in sin with a young Delilah, who, for an automobile, pulled the wool over the eyes of her elderly lover and her young bridegroom—until a penknife put an end to her philanderings!

The old undertaker had had a secret love affair with the young Delilah for several years. He was giving her money and had given her two automobiles. Apparently nobody in the community knew that he was mixed up with this young woman except the old family doctor. He had advised his patient to give up his sinful life; he warned him that he would come to grief if he didn't. He had told him that the strain of his guilt was breaking his nerves to pieces, and that he would finally collapse if he did not straighten up. The undertaker promised, but never quite found a place for repentance.

Finally a young man with a good position moved into the community, met the young woman, and soon married her, without the shadow of suspicion that she was a woman of sin!

At first the old undertaker seemed relieved; but within two weeks after she was married, this young Delilah was writing notes to her old fool of a lover, deceiving her stalwart, believing young husband, saying, "Where on earth were you yesterday? I wanted to see you so bad! I am tired of this married life. Could you possibly get the first payment on the car? . . . Please, Darling, give me another car!" This only two weeks after she had stood up before the preacher and had taken the vows of marriage to a high-minded, trusting young man who had fallen in love with her!

A few weeks passed. Her old lover seemed distraught by fear and worry. Young Delilah and he took a night trip to Washington, and there in a hotel room, at four o'clock in the morning, a woman's screams were heard! A hotel clerk was called, and when he pounded on the door from which the screams had issued, a tall, stoop-shouldered old man opened it. One of his arms hung limp, cut, slashed, bleeding. The clerk pushed in, and there on the floor lay Delilah, her head almost severed from her body with a broken-bladed penknife that lay at her side. "She's two-timed me for the last time," muttered her old lover!

The other day, convicted of murder, that old man was hustled off to spend the rest of his life behind prison bars as the punishment for his sin, while his wife and splendid daughters and sons bear the shame of his folly till their dying day!

Listen to me, young men, young women—all you sinners! *You can't do wrong and get away with it!* "Be sure your sin will find you out."

Take another horrible example. Several years ago Richard Bruno Hauptman was snapped into eternity in the electric chair for the most brutal crime in the history of our nation! For a long time it looked as if the kidnapper-murder of the Lindbergh baby never would be found out. But finally the case broke, and "diseased Nature" seemed to break forth in a strange eruption to disgorge the secret of Hauptman's guilt! All the evidence unquestionably fastened the crime on him.

But if Hauptman had never been found out in this world, and the murder of the Lindbergh baby had remained shrouded in mystery to the end of time, his sin would have been known to himself and to God, and it would have met him there at the final Judgment! *You cannot do wrong and get away with it.* "Be sure your sin will find you out."

II

How does sin find us out?

It finds us out in spite of the passing of time. When the trumpet of the Lord shall sound and time shall be no more, and the roll is called up yonder, we are going to be there, and we are going to have to give an account of ourselves to God. There can be no evading the scrutiny of Almighty God. If we wait ten million years, God will know all about us; he is keeping our records. The passing of time will not dim the records of our lives as lived here in the world.

Again, our sins will find us out in spite of our efforts to conceal them. The sons of Jacob, after they had sold Joseph into Egypt, kept their secret for twenty years. But their sin found them out in a most dramatic way!

A boy was playing with the paint where some workmen were doing some painting. He dropped one drop of red paint into a bucket of white paint. It scared him, and he wondered what to do. He grabbed a mixing stick and stirred the red into the bucket of white paint. He thought he had hidden it. But the trained eye of the painter detected the red cast in the paint the moment he returned. Just so, my friends, a little sin stirred into your lives makes their color different. You may think that you can hide your sins by stirring them into your daily conduct; but your sin will find you out. Your whole life will be shaded and blurred.

A tyrant commanded one of his slaves to make him a chain, without telling him what he was going to do with it. The slave went away and made the chain, and brought it to his master. He sent him back, saying, "Make it longer!" The slave went away and made it longer, and returned with it. Again the tyrant said, "Make it longer!" The slave went away and made it exceedingly long, and returned with it. Then the tyrant took the chain, forged by the slave, and bound him hand and foot and cast him into a dungeon. That is Satan's way with sinners: he tells you to sin, and sin, and sin, and all the time you are forging your own fetters that will hold you in the dungeon of your misery. "Be sure your sin will find you out."

In the next place, your sins will find you out in spite of any good deeds you may do to divert attention from them. There have been many hypocrites in the church. They steal the livery of God to serve Satan in. But most hypocrites are known by those who are closest to them. But if they should go all the way through the world without being detected, they would not fool God, nor themselves. They may be wolves in sheep's clothing; they may think they are getting away with it. But I tell you, my friends, your sin of hypocrisy will find you out.

There are men and women in this community who are fooling some of the people; but they are not fooling themselves, neither are they fooling God. They may be pulling the wool over the eyes of some who love them, but they cannot keep it up. Lincoln said, "You can fool some of the folks all the time, and all of the folks some of the time; but you can't fool all of the folks all of the time." Well, that is true, and I want to tell you sinners who are harboring secret sins in your lives that you cannot fool all the folks all the time, and you can't fool God at all, and you had better be done with sin! I warn you hypocrites here tonight that you are skating on thin ice; you are playing with fire; you are taking vipers into your bosom that will some day drive their fangs into your hearts and destroy you for this world and for the world to come.

Can a man take fire in his bosom and not be burned? Can a man step on hot coals and not burn his feet? Of course, he can't! And you sinners in the church, I tell you if you do not want to come to greater grief than you have ever known, you had better be done with sin. You can cover leprosy, or a cancer, with a soldier's uniform, but that uniform will not cure that leprosy, nor that cancer! A man in the church who is living a bad life is of all men most foolish. God looks not upon the outward appearance, but upon the heart. Some people are like crooked logs that have been sided up and dressed down till the outside appears fairly respectable, but their hearts are still crooked, like the hearts of the crooked logs! You must have straight hearts to meet the demands of God. God knows all about you, my friends. You had better look to your standing before God. You may be snatched away in your sin, but at any rate, you cannot fool God.

And I remind you that *sin will find you out in your whole life*. Sin destroys the bodies of men and women. I never see a red-nosed, blear-eyed, staggering, muttering, hiccoughing drunkard that I do not feel like calling all the young people of the community out to take a look at him, and saying to them, "There is what sin will do for you!" Liquor is a habit-forming drug, and it is almost as hard to overcome as any other drug habit. I am reminded of an incident that Doctor H. M. Wharton used to relate about an old drunk man that came into the church one night towards the close of the sermon, and came staggering down the aisle mumbling to the preacher that he wanted to say something. Some of the ushers grabbed the old soak and were about to lead him to the door when the pastor said, "Let him speak!" They held him upon his feet while the old man muttered, "Preacher, preach to the young people —tell them never to take the first—ich! first drink!— There's no use fooling with us old fellows—save the young folks—save the young folks!" It was a most impressive temperance speech. So I appeal to you young people: Do not take your first drink! If you take the first one you are liable to take the second, and the third, and so on to the end, and to a drunkard's grave!

But whiskey-drinking is not the only sin that harms the body. One of the tests of all amusements and habits is the question: Does it injure your health? If so, leave it alone. Anything that injures the body, which is the temple in which we live, is sinful and should be avoided. Immorality, crime, and dissipation bring distress, sorrow, suffering, desolation, and death. Prisons and penitentiaries and asylums are but the junk piles of human wreckage produced by sin! All the world knows the story of the sinful life of Byron, the English poet. In the Library of Trinity College, Cambridge, there is a remarkable statue of that young genius. Looking at it from one angle, people exclaim,

"What a genius he was! What a fine expression and noble face!" Then the guide takes you to another side, from which you see only a scowl and a dreadful leer. The guide explains by saying, "The artist pictures in this statue two characters—the great genius, the towering intellect—yet the enormous mass of sin that was in his soul." The whole world is familiar with the tragic ruin to which his sinful life brought him. He was famous, but he allowed sin to ruin him. He died in his early thirties, moaning,

> My days are in the yellow leaf;
> The worm, the canker, and the grief,
> Are mine alone!

Our sin will find us out!

And sin finds us out in our minds. Sin actually beclouds the brain, dims the vision, and causes moral colorblindness! There are many young people today whose consciences never seem to bother them, and who never blush. They glory in their shame; they think it smart to sin!

The Bible says, however, "Woe unto them that call evil good, and good evil." There is no other tragedy quite so appalling as for a man to lose his sense of right and wrong. Here and there we find people like that. Some people ridicule the Bible conception of sin; they say that sin is only a "cultural lag," or a "defect," or a "gap between what we are and what we think we should be," or a "minus sign which will disappear as we grow up." But sin is more than any of these. Sin is a breach of personal relations with God; it is unbelief; it is everything that is contrary to the will of God.

The result of it is spiritual death, which is separation from God. And sin finds us out by producing in us a state of mind that leads to rebellion against God. The carnal mind is enmity against God: it repulses God's loving advances, resists his control, and shrinks from his holiness.

Sin also finds us out in our homes. There is nothing that plays such havoc with our homes as does sin. Sin ruined the home of the first couple in the Garden of Eden, and the transgression of Adam and Eve passed on to their children, and to the race.

You remember how sin worked out in the life of Adam and Eve's sons, Cain and Abel. There is no more terrible story of sin in the annals of human life than that of Cain and Abel. You recall that when Cain was angered with his brother and slew him, the Lord said to Cain: "Where is Abel thy brother?" and Cain replied: "I know not: am I my brother's keeper?" You see he lied about it; he denied that he knew anything about it, or that he had any responsibility for his brother. But did he get away with it? Not at all! God plied him with another question—"What hast thou done? The voice of thy brother's blood crieth unto me from the ground." That is the way of sin! If we lie about it, or deny it, somehow the very earth seems to cry out against us! Adam and Eve's sin was perpetuated in their children, and Cain wailed out, "My punishment is greater than I can bear." But that day he went out to be a vagabond and a fugitive in the earth! Cain's sin found him out and ruined his life. My sinner friends, your sins will find you out and ruin your lives. And when sin comes into the life of any

member of a family, that home is hurt—that home is
made wretched.   Nearly every broken home that we
know anything about was broken by death, or by sin!
They are the two great destroyers of our homes—*sin
and death!*   Sin played havoc with the home of Adam
and Eve, and it destroyed and ruined any prospects of
a happy home for both Cain and Abel, and it will do
the same for every home in the world!

And look at what sin did for the home of Jacob!
Jacob, when he was a young man, decided that he could
do wrong and get away with it.   He deceived his old
father and supplanted his brother.   He showed himself a cheat and a swindler by stealing his brother's
birthright and his father's blessing.   But did he get
pleasure out of it?   Did he get away with it?   You
remember how he ran away from home, and married,
and reared a family of children, and how his children
broke his heart!   You remember how Jacob loved
Joseph, how his heart was wrapped up in that boy! But
his joy was not for long, for his other sons became
jealous of Joseph, and decided to make way with him.
They first decided to put him in a pit and let him starve
to death; then they decided to sell him to some Midian-
ites, to be resold into Egypt as a slave, which they did.
Then they took Joseph's coat and drenched it in blood
and took it home to their father and told him that a
wild beast had devoured their little brother, and that
they did not know anything about it except that they
had found his bloody coat.   It nearly broke the old
father's heart—but he was reaping what he had sown
in young manhood.   He had mistreated his brother;
now his sons were mistreating their brother.   He had

deceived his father by wrapping his hands up with a kid's skin to make them seem hairy; now his sons were deceiving him by bringing home their little brother's coat drenched in the blood of a kid that they had slain. Isaac, Jacob's father, wept over Jacob's sins; now Jacob wept over the sins of his own sons! Ah, my friends, sin turns our homes into hells on earth! Nothing in all the world so destroys the peace and happiness of homes as does sin in the lives of the parents or the children!

Look around you and you will be surprised how all the unhappiness that you see in the homes of the people is due to sin! Sin finds us out in our homes!

III

We have seen that sin finds us out, and we have seen how it finds us out, yet the half has not been told. But now I want to appeal to you to be done with sin!

"Be not deceived; God is not mocked: for whatsoever a man soweth, that shall he also reap."

"The wages of sin is death."

"The stars in their courses fought against Sisera."

"The name of the wicked shall rot."

"These shall go away into everlasting punishment."

These are some of the great pronouncements of the Bible about the penalty of sin. My sinner friends, are you keeping bad company? Remember that "the companion of fools shall be destroyed."

Are you trifling with dishonesty? Are you harboring any known sin in your life? Are you cherishing any secret sin in your heart? If so, I tell you, "your sin will find you out"; and I plead with you to be done with it tonight. "Sin produces moral ulcers. A festering character is worse than a festering body. A rotten soul is worse than a rotten body."

And are you hardening your heart against the call of God? If so, I plead with you to cease your rebellion. "It is hard for you to kick against the goads." God wants you to be done with sin, and he assures you that if you will turn away from sin and accept Christ as the Master of your life, he will count that as righteousness for you. That is all that you have to do to be saved, to be free from your sin, to be cleansed of all unrighteousness and made right in God's sight.

Turn your back upon your sins, and come to Christ and be saved. He is your only hope. If you think you can ever save yourself by your own wisdom, by your own moral efforts, by living a good life according to your own mind apart from Christ, you are doomed to disappointment and to death. The struggle with evil in your own strength is illustrated in the Laocoon of art. Probably you have seen the picture of the old priest of Apollo, Laocoon, and his sons, encoiled by serpents, and suffering the agonies of strangulation. The priest-father is vainly endeavoring to disengage himself and his children from the coils of the serpents; but he is helpless and hopeless; and sinks at last into despair!

That is the tragic picture of man trying to save himself by his own wisdom and strength! No man has ever been able to save himself by his own power or wisdom. That is why Christ came. He came to rescue us from the coils of the serpents of sin. He is our only hope. Put your trust in him tonight. "Be sure your sin will find you out."

VIII

AN ENDURING EXAMPLE

But one thing is needful: and Mary hath chosen that good part, which shall not be taken away from her.—LUKE 10: 42.

And Jesus said, Let her alone; why trouble ye her? She hath wrought a good work on me. . . . She hath done what she could. —MARK 14: 6, 8.

Verily I say unto you, Wheresoever this gospel shall be preached throughout the whole world, this also that she hath done shall be spoken of for a memorial of her.—MARK 14: 9.

Sometime ago I was reading these passages about Mary of Bethany, and as I read them, three statements seemed to stand out in bold emphasis: "Mary hath chosen the good part." . . . "She hath wrought a good work on me." . . . and "Wheresoever this gospel shall be preached throughout the whole world, this also that she hath done shall be spoken of for a memorial of her."

As I read those expressions, my heart thrilled with the exquisite beauty of the phrases, and I mused to myself—"Her wise choice!—Her good work!—Her enduring fame!" I felt the thrill of a new creation! A new sermon had come to me!

So I desire to think with you for a little while about Mary of Bethany as one who made the wisest choice one can make, and as one who did the best work one can do, and as one who won an enduring fame.

I

Think of *Mary's wise choice!* Jesus had stopped by for a little visit in the home of Martha and Mary. Mary sat at his feet and heard his word, while Martha was cumbered about much serving. So Martha came to Jesus, and said, "Lord, dost thou not care that my sister hath left me alone? bid her therefore that she help me." Jesus replied, "Martha, Martha, thou art careful and troubled about many things: but one thing is needful: and Mary hath chosen that good part, which shall not be taken away from her."

Jesus was placed in a delicate situation: he was a guest in the home, and there was a sharp difference of opinion between Mary and Martha. But Jesus seized upon that moment to teach one of the greatest lessons of his life!

Martha was cumbered about much serving, while Mary sat at the Lord's feet and heard his words. In those two women Jesus saw the two great attitudes of life: Mary was putting the emphasis of life upon spiritual and eternal things, while Martha was putting it upon material and temporal things. Jesus set those two attitudes in clear contrast by the example of those two sisters, and made them the symbols of two great philosophies of life,—Martha representing those who make the world of "things" the end of life, and Mary representing those who put God and his kingdom first!

We all have to face these two great alternatives and make our choice between them. We are compelled to make the choice of putting spiritual and eternal things first, or of putting material and temporal things first. It happened that Mary set the right example for us and for all people for all time; and Jesus was ready to commend her for her wise choice, and to hold her up as an enduring example.

There were two reasons why Mary's choice was wise:

First, her choice was wise because it was *needful*. In his desire to set Martha right about her attitude, Jesus said: "Martha, Martha, thou art careful and troubled about many things: but one thing is *needful*." Jesus meant to say to Martha that in the light of eternity, there is but one thing that is absolutely necessary, and that is to have the right attitude of heart and mind— to be right in one's attitude towards God and towards eternal things. He was meaning to say to Martha what he said to his disciples in the Sermon on the Mount,— that spiritual things should come first,—by which he meant that she should realize that she was a creature of two worlds, not merely an animal to be fed and made comfortable. He did not mean to imply that food and clothing were not necessary, but that we should seek first the kingdom of God and his righteousness. It was the same lesson that he taught in the great Sermon when he said, "No man can serve two masters: for either he will hate the one, and love the other; or else he will hold to one, and despise the other. Ye cannot serve God and mammon. Therefore I say unto you, Be not anxious for your life, what ye shall eat, or what ye shall drink; nor yet for your body, what ye shall put on. Is not the life more than the food, and the body than the raiment? . . . *But seek ye first his kingdom, and his righteousness; and all these things shall be added unto you.*"

One's attitude towards Christ settles this matter. Mary, in sitting at Jesus' feet and listening to his words, exemplified the great choice that every soul should make; it is the supremely important choice of time and eternity, the one absolutely needful choice for every soul!

This choice properly relates us to our Saviour; it sets him at the center of our lives; it crowns him as our King. This is needful; without it we are lost; we are in the dark, we know not whither we go, we are not properly related to God. The rich young ruler came to Jesus and bowing before him said: "Good Master, what must I do to inherit eternal life?" Jesus reminded him first of the Commandments; and when the young man assured him that he had observed them from his youth, Jesus told him that he lacked one thing, and that was to go and sell all his property and give it to the poor, and come follow him. But the young man could not find it in his heart to do what Jesus told him to do, but went away sorrowful, for he was very rich. That young man had everything except the one thing that was needful. He possessed fortune, social position, culture, elegance of manner, courtesy, wealth, morality— all these things! Yet he lacked one thing—the spirit of Mary who "sat at the Lord's feet and heard his word." Mary had sincerely come to the place where Christ was first in her life. But there was something utterly pathetic about that young man who had so much, but lacked the main thing!

Many years ago, when Doctor John A. Broadus was a student at the University of Virginia, he had a brilliant schoolmate who was not a Christian. Broadus prayed for him and sought all the time they were in the university to lead him to Christ, but to no avail. Finally the time of graduation was at hand, and they were to part, maybe forever. According to the custom in those days, the two young men were exchanging autographs. Broadus inscribed in his friend's little book just three words in Greek and closed it up and handed it back to him. Those three words were: *Hen se husterei,*—"one thing thou lackest," the words of Jesus to the rich young ruler, as recorded in Mark 10:21. Years later, when Doctor Broadus had become famous as one of the greatest scholars and preachers of all time, he received word from his old friend of university days, then a successful physician in Texas, telling him that he had at last found the "one thing" he lacked—he had found Christ as his Saviour! The three little words, *Hen se husterei,*—"one thing thou lackest,—" had at last brought forth the desired harvest! My sinner friends, you lack one thing, if you have never made the wise choice that Mary made; you lack Christ as your Saviour; he is absolutely needful, and, in comparison, nothing else matters very greatly!

Again, Mary's choice was wise because she had chosen "that good part" that should not be "taken away from her." Jesus was stating in that remark a profound truth. Paul stated it later in this way: "We look not at the things which are seen, but at the things that are not seen: for the things that are seen are temporal; but the things that are not seen are eternal."

Mary's choice of sitting at the feet of Jesus and listening to his words *symbolized her grasp of eternal things!* She saw in Christ the reality and eternity of the unseen world, and because she did so, Jesus commended her and held her up as an enduring example of wisdom and spiritual insight. She had apprehended "that good part" which should not be taken away from her!

How different this is from any earthly possession! If we lay up treasures upon earth, we know that moth and rust will consume them, or else thieves will break through and steal them, or death will soon drag us away from them. It is a certain fact that no matter how much of this world's goods we may possess, we cannot carry any of it with us into eternity—beyond the portals of death. If Jesus taught anything, he taught the folly of making mammon our God. Think of Dives, who spent his whole life heaping together a great fortune, to the neglect of his soul; and when death came, he was ushered into eternity, totally unprepared for it; and in eternity he was of all beings most to be pitied. He was in torment, and prayed for one drop of water to cool his tongue! On the other hand, think of Lazarus, the poor beggar, who died at the rich man's gate. He was poor while he lived in the world, but was rich towards God; and in eternity he came into possessions far better than all the silver and gold of this world!

And how different it is from *earthly fame* for which some sell their souls! If we win fame here in this world, it invariably stales or brings tragedy and heartbreak. Col. Chas. A. Lindbergh is now living a life of self-imposed exile because life in America became unbearable for him. Once the supremely famous man of the world, almost idolized by an admiring public, he soon became the victim of all the harpies of the world when they began tearing his heart out; and the vanity of all earthly glory was horribly dramatized in the kidnapping and murder of his little boy! Not all earthly glory ends in such tragedy; but it has a way of staling and turning to dust and ashes, leaving life strangely bereft of pleasure! And the more of earthly glory one enjoys today, the bitterer the dregs of disillusionment tomorrow!

And even *human love* may prove false and disappointing, with broken hearts and shattered dreams as the fearful consequence. But no such tragedy ever befalls those who link their lives with Christ. When all other helpers fail, Christ, the Great Friend, remains faithful! It is wise to choose such a Friend. It is wise to sit at his feet—to put first things first—so that neither life nor death, nor things present nor things to come, nor powers nor principalities, nor any other creature shall be able to separate us from the love of God which is in Christ Jesus our Lord!

Mary made this wise choice; all this is included in her choice when she put first things first, and sat at the feet of Jesus! She chose the good part that should not be taken away from her. It was the wisest choice one could make!

II

Let us look now at *Mary's "good work!"* Her wise choice was followed by her good work for Christ. In Mark 14: 3-9, we have the story of Christ's anointment by Mary.

You recall the circumstances. It was only two days before the crucifixion. The Jews were plotting his death. Jesus had gone out to Bethany to spend the night with his friends, Martha, Mary, and Lazarus, along with some of his disciples. The shadow of the

Cross lay upon his path, and the weight of the world's sin was on his heart. Probably, as they sat at the table, Jesus had told them plainly that he was going to be put to death. It was a sad, sad evening!

Mark tells us that "as he sat at meat, there came a woman having an alabaster box of ointment of spikenard very precious," and unsealed it "and poured it on his head." When she did that, some "had indignation within themselves, and said, Why was this waste of the ointment made? For it might have been sold for more than three hundred pence, and have been given to the poor. And they murmured against her." It was then that Jesus took her part, saying, "Let her alone; why trouble ye her? *She hath wrought a good work on me.* For ye have the poor with you always, and whensoever ye will ye may do them good; but me ye have not always. *She hath done what she could:* she is come aforehand to anoint my body to the burying."

This is the simple record of one of the sublimest deeds ever performed in the world, brought into heavenly relief against a background of human blindness and greed, unsurpassed in human depravity!

When Mary poured that precious ointment on the Lord's head, some "murmured against her," suggesting that it was foolish for her to "waste" her precious treasure of pure nard,—that it might have been sold for three hundred pence—probably five hundred dollars —and given to the poor. But Jesus took her part, and commended her for her loving thoughtfulness and service to him in the hour of his great spiritual anguish and pain. Jesus said that it was "a good work"—that

she had done "what she could"—and that instead of
being blamed for it, she should be commended. It was
an immortal deed!

What was there about that act that made it so great?
What was there about it that caused Christ to commend
her so highly for it? What made it such "a good
work"?

It is important that we analyze this act of Mary's,
for the very things that commended her act to Christ
in such a remarkable way are the things that must make
every act of service acceptable to him.

First, it was *a good work* because it represented *self-
denial*. It was a work that required a great sacrifice
on her part. Nobody knows how much Mary prized
that box of precious ointment. Her mother may have
left it to her. It was "very precious." And then it
had commercial value that seems to us utterly fabulous.
But in that hour, evidently when her heart had been
deeply moved by the heavenly goodness of her Lord, and
by the thought that he was soon to suffer death for
the sins of the world, she had to do something for him!
What could she do? She could only do as we sometimes have to do when we can only send a bunch of
flowers to our friends. She could not express what was
in her heart with words; she could not go out and
destroy his enemies; but, at whatever cost, she could
show him that her heart was as his heart; that she was
with him in his trouble. She would do that, even if it
required the sacrifice of her most precious treasure!
So she went away and brought the alabaster box and
unsealed it, and poured its contents on the head of her
Lord. Now the first thing about that act that made

it so heavenly, so remarkable, was that it required self-denial on her part. She loved her precious treasure, assuredly; maybe she had had other plans as to what she would do with it; but now in a great need, and in a great crisis in the life of her Lord, she would make *any sacrifice in the world* to help her Master bear his great burden. You see what it all meant; it was a self-denying, sacrificial act, and that made it an act that Christ approved and commended!

We have never done a truly "good work" in the service of our Lord until we have done something that required some self-denial on our part. Sometime ago I was preaching about *giving,* and made the statement that nobody ever tasted the joy of giving until he had *given sacrificially*—till he had to forego something he would like to have for himself in order to give. After the service, a young man of considerable wealth came to speak to me in front of the pulpit. He was deeply impressed with what I had said. Then, in a most earnest and friendly way, he said, "I was just wondering as you were preaching whether I had ever in my life known the joy of giving; for I never have had to do without anything that I wanted in order to give what I have given. In fact," he continued, "I do not know how I could do that without giving away so much that it would injure my business. But," he proceeded, "I was thinking of another way that I could make some self-denial. I can do it by giving a part of my time! I have no more time than anybody else; and I was just thinking if that would meet the requirement, I would tell you that if I can be of any service to the church by giving my time, I want you to know I am ready to do anything, or to go anywhere, and give as much of my time as is necessary to help our church and the cause of Christ. *I want to taste the joy of self-denial!"* My friends, that young man had apprehended the meaning of Mary's "good work." I think it was one of the finest speeches I ever heard a young man make.

I shall never forget a heavenly vision that I saw at Wake Forest College in my student days there. Miss Sophie Lanneau, the daughter of the venerable professor of Astronomy and Applied Mathematics, had just finished Meredith College, and was leaving for New York to sail for China as a missionary. It had been noised abroad that she would be leaving that afternoon, and many of the students had gone down to the depot to witness her departure. It was in the springtime and the huge magnolia trees were in bloom; the grass on the campus was fresh, through which the gravel walks wound from Faculty Avenue down to the depot. No lovelier people ever trod those sacred paths than those three who came walking arm in arm together down from their home among the elms, to meet the train that late afternoon—Miss Sophie in the middle, her venerable father, tall and handsome, on her right; and her dear, gentle, little mother on her left—walking in the gathering shadows of a golden sunset, with thoughts and feelings too deep for words! I stood at a distance and watched them, then followed, and saw the train roll into the station; saw the fond parents tenderly kiss their radiant daughter good-bye, realizing that they might never see her again; saw the old train pull out, and wind around the curve to the north and out of sight. To me it was one of the most beautiful pictures I ever saw; if I were an artist I would paint it as it impressed me.

A moment after the train had vanished over the hill, however, the boys broke into a spontaneous expression of their feelings. Some were saying: "I don't see any sense in her wanting to go to China!" Others said: "I don't see how she could leave such a father and mother and such a home!" Still others said: "We don't see why she wants to waste her life like that when she could stay at home and enjoy life and have a good time!"

Such was the blind babble! My mind turned to this incident in the life of Mary, and to those who "had indignation within themselves, and said, Why was this waste of the ointment made?" Mary's work was a good work because it was a work of self-denial; and so it is with all truly good work for Christ. *It must be sacrificial!*

In the second place, Mary's work was *good because it was an expression of love and gratitude*. The Master had done much for Mary. She had sat at his feet and had heard his words of grace and truth which had meant life to her; and the Master had been with her in the deepest sorrows of her life, the death of her only brother; and, marvelous to say, Jesus had raised him up with a mighty miracle, and had restored him to his place in the Bethany home! There was such a warmth of love and gratitude in Mary's heart that she felt that she never could do anything for the Lord that would adequately express her heart-felt gratitude for all his goodness and kindness to her. So her work for the Lord was an expression of her love and gratitude!

Nothing is baser than ingratitude, and there is nothing finer and better in human life than appreciation and gratitude! "It is a good thing to give thanks unto the Lord." Mary did not have to strain her affections to bring forth the alabaster box of ointment; it was the spontaneous expression of her heart. There wasn't much that she could do; but what she could do, that she did. She wanted to show her love and gratitude; and, in the only way left to her, she did it; and it was a good work because it was the genuine, unstrained expression of two of the noblest attributes of the soul.

Tennyson describes Mary's feelings as she thought of the raising of her brother, and as she came to anoint the Lord. He says:

> Her eyes are homes of silent prayer,
>   Nor other thought her mind admits
>   But, he was dead, and there he sits,
> And He that brought him back is there.
>
> Then one deep love doth supersede
>   All other, when her ardent gaze
>   Roves from the living brother's face,
> And rests upon the Life indeed.
>
> All subtle thought, all curious fears,
>   Borne down by gladness so complete,
>   She bows, she bathes the Saviour's feet
> With costly spikenard and with tears.
>
> Thrice blest whose lives are faithful prayers,
>   Whose loves in higher love endure;
>   What souls possess themselves so pure,
> Or is there blessedness like theirs?

Yes, the thing that made her work so wonderfully good was that it was a work of love and rapturous gratitude. And all such work is good, no matter what it costs!

Then there was something else that made her anointing of the Lord a good work: it was good because it was so *timely!* Translated into present-day terminology, Mary threw her flowers in the Lord's pathway instead of keeping them to put upon his grave. That was what the Lord meant when he said, "She hath done what she could: she is come aforehand to anoint my body to the burying."

Mary did not keep her precious alabaster box of ointment for his cold, dead body; she broke it and poured it upon his head as a token of love and understanding, of sympathy and cheer, while he could benefit by it; while he needed the courage and power to go forward in his redemptive purpose. She knew that he was already passing into the shadow of death; she knew that there were cruel enemies plotting his crucifixion; she knew his "soul was exceeding sorrowful, even unto death." She came while she could, and poured her precious ointment on his head. What a beautiful, what a touching scene! What a timely act of kindness!

As I contemplate this beautiful deed, I know that all about us, every day, there are those whose lives could be made infinitely more bearable, more sweet, more beautiful, if only all of us would seize our opportunities as they pass, and do what we could to lighten their loads and cheer them along the way. Everywhere we turn, we find husbands whose lives are one long grind of dreary toil for their families, with never a flower thrown in their way by those who should make life sweet for them; everywhere we find wives with crushed and lonely hearts who would be happy if they could find a few flow-ers in their path once in a while—a few little thoughtful deeds and kind words; but they go through life bowed down and broken-hearted, when somebody could make them happy with a little bit of understanding love! There are whole families of children who never know the blessedness of a happy home, because father and mother have not learned the magic of gentle and kind words, and controlled tempers; and, saddest of all, I have seen fond parents, who have worked themselves almost to death for their children from their birth to maturity, neglected, forgotten, left lonely in their de-clining years, cast off when they are old, because of the cruel neglect of their own children!

Ah, my friends, the good deed of Mary in doing what she could to ease the pain and sorrow of the Mas-ter's heart as he faced Calvary, is a lesson we all need to learn! We ought not to keep the alabaster boxes of our love and tenderness sealed up till our friends are dead. We ought to fill their lives with sweetness; we ought to speak approving and cheering words while their hearts can be thrilled and made happy by them. The kind things we mean to do or say when they are gone should be said or done before they leave us. The flowers we mean to send for their funerals we should send to brighten and sweeten their homes. We all know that this is the good thing to do, and it is a tragedy that we will not do as well as we know.

The funeral of a prominent man was conducted some-time ago in a small town in North Carolina. The lead-ing man of that village, the banker, had met with reverses, and had lost all the money entrusted to him by his friends and neighbors; and in sorrow and despair he had killed himself. All who knew him loved him; and, even in death and the loss of their money in his bank, they still loved him. At his funeral the whole front of the auditorium of the church was filled with flowers. Never had so many flowers been seen at a funeral in that community. In the course of his remarks as he conducted the funeral, the minister said: "We have a profusion of flowers here today. I know they are tokens of your love for this friend. But you waited too long . . . they came too late. . . . Oh, that we had brought a few of them last week! If we had, we should not be here today!"

Tears filled the eyes of all the people present, and sobs were in their hearts. The preacher had told them the truth! Probably they would have brought some of those flowers to him the week before if they had known the agony through which he was passing; but that is just the point—*we are so slow to understand,* and so prone to wait! Mary did not have to be told that Jesus needed sympathy, love, understanding; *her soul was awake,* and she saw for herself, and she did what the occasion required.

So we see that Mary's work was *good* because it involved self-denial, because it was a work of love and gratitude, and because it was a golden deed well-timed. What a wonderful example of how to do good!

III

Now, in conclusion, notice *Mary's enduring fame!* Horace said of his achievements as a poet, "I have completed a monument more lasting than bronze, and more sublime than the regal elevation of pyramids, which neither the wasting shower, the unavailing north wind, or an innumerable succession of years, and the flight of seasons, shall be able to demolish." But Mary, in the good work of breaking the alabaster box and anointing the Master's head the night before his passion and death, erected a more enduring memorial than Horace produced in his book of poems.

Jesus said, "Verily I say unto you, Wheresoever this gospel shall be preached throughout the whole world, this also that she has done shall be spoken of for a memorial of her." Hers was an immortal deed, and was ordained of Christ to be spoken of forever as a memorial of her, and as an example to all who should come after her!

May we all make the choice she made, and do the same sort of good work; and if we do, we shall in no wise lose our reward!

IX

THE FIRST FIVE MINUTES AFTER DEATH

And it came to pass, that the beggar died, and was carried away by the angels into Abraham's bosom: and the rich man also died, and was buried. And in Hades he lifted up his eyes, being in torments, and seeth Abraham afar off, and Lazarus in his bosom.—LUKE 16: 22, 23.

My subject tonight is "The First Five Minutes After Death." I realize that some may say at the very beginning of this message that nobody knows what is going to take place in the experience of the soul immediately after death. But that attitude does not take into account the plain teachings of the New Testament, nor the profound interest that most people have in the question of the Great Hereafter.

I was called to the hospital not long ago to see an old man who was passing into the valley of the shadow of death. I did not know just why he had called me. He had been a mighty man physically, and I found him, like a stricken old giant, lying helpless, and fully conscious that he had come to the end of all earthly resources. He was magnificent in his courage, deliberation, and calmness; yet there was something ghastly about him, as of the death-struggle of a giant. He was more than eighty years old, an old Union soldier, with a deep, resonant voice. His eyes were light blue—clear, searching—with a bit of frantic glare in them, as if he saw that he was in the grip of a mortal enemy.

After a few words of greeting, I asked him if there was anything special that he wanted to talk about, to which he replied in a deep, quavering voice: "Yes—I want you to tell me about the Hereafter—I know that I can't stay here much longer—and I don't know much about how the next world is going to be. My father died when I was just a little boy—I scarcely remember him—My mother worked hard to feed us children—but she couldn't teach us. I left home as soon as I was big enough to work—then the war came on, and I joined the army. I never was taught about the Bible and religion. Then when the war was over, I worked here and there, and never went to church much—I joined the church after I was married, but I didn't attend much —I ought to have done better. So here I am, facing whatever there is in the next world!—I want you to tell me how it is going to be over there!"

I sat down and explained the plan of salvation to him, and how eagerly he listened! And how glad he was to accept it, and claim Christ as his Saviour! Then I read many passages of the Bible to him. I read the first part of the fourteenth chapter of John, and the Twenty-third Psalm, and many passages about the blessedness of the dead that die in the Lord. I read him those verses from the fifth chapter of Second Corinthians, "For we know that if our earthly house of this tabernacle were dissolved, we have a building of God, an house not made with hands, eternal in the heavens." Then I read from the twenty-first chapter of the Book of Revelation, "And I saw a new heaven and a new earth: for the first heaven and the first earth were passed away. . . . And God shall wipe away all tears from their eyes; and there shall be no more death, neither sorrow, nor crying, neither shall there be any more pain: for the former things are passed away." The old man drank in all those passages with the eagerness of a wounded soldier on a hot day drinking water on the battlefield. He kept breaking in as I read: "That's wonderful!—And that's the way it's going to be over there?—Oh, how I wish I had known that!" I kept on assuring him that he could claim all those blessed passages as God's promises to him because of his faith in Christ, and on the basis of sincere repentance. Never before had I seen the truth of the Bible bring such light and hope and comfort!

You may not be interested in my subject tonight; but there will come a time when you will be more interested in what is going to happen to you the first five minutes after death than in any other subject in all the world; and it is wise and well to begin thinking about it now. I do not claim any unusual understanding of these matters; all that I propose to tell you about the first five minutes after death is derived directly from the New Testament, and mainly from the story of the Rich Man and Lazarus, as recorded here in the sixteenth chapter of Luke. So let it be understood clearly that I am presenting no new theories about the life beyond the grave, but the plain teaching of the New Testament, as understood by most Christians.

Before entering specifically, however, upon the discussion of the subject of the first five minutes after death, let us glance at the scheme of things as they lie out before us, according to God's plan. The big events in God's unfolding plan of the ages are these: First, there is death. We know that all must die— unless the end of the world should come before our span of life is over. We are taught, however, to be constantly watching for the return of the Lord, and if he comes before we die, then we shall not see death, but shall be changed, and made into immortal beings without tasting death. This was a strong hope with Christians in the early centuries and is a blessed hope with many at the present moment. But death is one of the great certainties with us, if the present order continues. Then comes the intermediate state—the state of the disembodied spirits of all men between death and the Resurrection. At the end of the present dispensation, Christ will return, and the dead will be raised. That will be the Great Resurrection. Then follows the final Judgment, when the righteous will be separated from the wicked, and the wicked shall be cast into hell where they shall be punished forever and forever; while, on the other hand, the righteous shall be led away into heaven, into eternal blessedness, into the kingdom prepared for them from the foundation of the world. These are the great events before us, according to the teachings of the New Testament. How important, then, that we should make ready for them, and be found on God's right hand in the Great Judgment!

But what about the dead the first five minutes, or immediately after death? How is it going to be with them? Where are we going to be, and what will we be thinking about? and how will we be faring? These are the questions before us; and Jesus gave us the answer to all these in the story of the Rich Man and Lazarus. I ask you, therefore, to think with me about these two cases—Dives and Lazarus. Dives symbolizes for us the plight of the sinner the first five minutes after death, and Lazarus symbolizes for us the state of the redeemed the first five minutes after death.

I

Now let us follow, first, the Rich Man, the sinner man, the lost man, out beyond the portals of death, and see how things were with him immediately after he passed over. If we follow him and observe what he was thinking, and how he was feeling, and how he was faring, we shall see how it is going to be with all lost souls who go out to meet God unprepared.

First, you will observe that he died. That was the door through which he passed into eternity. I merely mention this to remind you, sinner friends, that death is the door into eternity through which you must shortly pass. Dives *died,* and he died before he expected to die! He died without making preparation to die—a thing, in all probability, he never expected to do. Most likely he thought he would have time a-plenty later. But he waited too long and was snatched away in sin, unprepared to meet God.

We notice, also, that he "was buried." The language suggests that he was given a great funeral. Most likely that is what happened. He had a great deal of this world's goods, and rich sinners as a rule are given great funerals.

But when he was buried, that was as far as his wealth could do him any good. He left it all behind, "and in Hades he lifted up his eyes, being in torments." Now let me explain that word Hades. There has been a great deal of confusion in our thinking about hell because the King James translation has the word "hell" here in our text, instead of "Hades." Because the translators put the word "hell" here in this passage, a great many people have been misled into thinking that the soul goes to its eternal habitation immediately after death. But that is not true. Dives did not go to hell, but to Hades; and Hades is not the eternal abode of the wicked; it is the abode of the wicked between death and the Resurrection. This Rich Man was not in hell, but in Hades. Hell will be the home of the wicked after the Resurrection and the Judgment. Let us keep these facts in our minds. So, "in Hades he lifted up his eyes, being in torments." There are two thoughts here:

Observe that "he lifted up his eyes." That means that he woke up, he got his eyes open. My sinner friends, that man never seemed to get his eyes open until he woke up in the lost world! There are many now, some in this congregation perhaps, who are dozing through life, and never are going to wake up till they wake up in the lost world. But they certainly will wake up then, and lift up their drooping eyelids. I plead with you not to make the mistake that Dives made!

And he was "in torments." He did not have to wait for vast ages to roll by before he began to suffer; he was not asleep; he was not in a stupor; his eyes were wide open, and he was fully aware of all that was going on, and he was "in torments." It was a torment as of burning, scorching flame, with all its anguish, and indescribable pain!

Then what did he do? He did exactly what you will do, my sinner friends. He began to pray: he converted Hades into a prayer meeting! In Hades he lifted up his eyes, being in torments, and he looked away across a great gulf and saw Abraham, and Lazarus in his bosom; and then he cried out, saying, "Father Abraham, have mercy on me, and send Lazarus, that he may dip the tip of his finger in water, and cool my tongue; for I am tormented in this flame."

You see what is going to happen to a lost person the first five minutes after he dies. He will be in Hades, and he will be in torments, and he will be praying. And here again we have two most solemn facts:

He will first pray for himself. He will be praying for some good man or woman to come over from Paradise and bring him a little water to cool his tongue. And if you die in your sins, my friends, you, too, will first of all pray for yourself. You will pray for relief from your anguish and woe. You will be realizing as you never could realize in this world the awful sufferings of the lost world! And you will pray for relief from your sufferings! But the sad part of it is that, though you pray, though you pray for only a few drops of water, you will not get even so small a favor! When the Rich Man prayed for water to cool his tongue, he was reminded of his own rotten sinfulness, and of how he let people suffer all about him while he was in the world, without lifting his little finger to do one thing in the world for them! God said to him: "Son, remember that thou in thy lifetime receivedst thy good things, and likewise Lazarus evil things: but now he is comforted, and thou art tormented." That was the answer that he got when he asked God to give him a few drops of water! My sinner friends, he prayed, but he did not get what he asked for; he waited too late!

But when he found that he could not get any relief

for himself; that he could not get any water to cool his tongue, what was his next thought? He was shown that he was not there for a short time, a mere unpleasant vacation, or a brief chastisement, but that he was lost forever, and that there was no chance for him ever to escape from the doom which he had chosen.

When he prayed for God to send Lazarus that he might dip his finger in water and cool his tongue, God reminded him that there was no crossing over from one place to the other! Abraham, as God's spokesman, speaking from Paradise, said, "Between us . . . there is a great gulf fixed: so that they which would pass from hence to you cannot; neither can they pass to us, that would come from thence." That was to say, there is no salvation after death. That is one of the great horrors of the lost world: there will be no chance to change from Hades to Paradise! My sinner friends, this is a most important truth: if you die in your sins, there will be no place of change after death: as the tree falls so must it lie! That was one of the great discoveries that Dives made the first five minutes after he died: he realized that he was fixed in eternal suffering, with not one particle of chance in all eternity for him to change his condition!

Well, when he found that there was no chance of any relief for him, and that he was doomed forever to suffer, what did he do? He did just what all lost souls will do: he tried to get a message back to his loved ones still living to warn them not to come to that place of torment! He said, "I pray thee therefore, father, that thou wouldest send him to my father's house: for I have five brethren; that he may testify

unto them, lest they also come to this place of torment." Yes, sir, he began to pray for his five brothers
back in the world lest they also should come to that
place of torment! And that is what all you sinners will
do if you die in your sins. You never have prayed here,
even for yourselves, but out there in Hades you will
pray! Dives prayed for his lost brothers.

But his prayer was not answered. God told him that
they had Moses and the prophets, and that they ought
to hear them: and, if they would not hear them, they
would not be persuaded, though one rose from the dead!

To me there is something profoundly pathetic in the
thought of a lost soul in Hades praying for lost friends
back in the world! It shows us that if there is a lost
man here tonight who has ever had a friend to die in
his sins, that friend is praying in the lost world for you
here! He is trying to get a message back to you from
that place of sorrow and woe, to head you off and keep
you from coming to that place of torment! But God
says to you, even as he said to Dives, that he will not
send a messenger to you from the lost world, nor from
Paradise. God is saying to you, sinners, "They have
Moses (the Bible) and the prophets (the preachers):
let them hear them." God knows that if you, lost men
and women, will not hear what the Bible and the preachers have to say to you, you would not be persuaded,
though one rose from the dead and came and stood in
your midst to warn you! And God knew what he was
talking about; he knew what was in the heart of men.
He was telling you the hard, honest truth, sinner man!
I am trying to deliver God's message of warning to you
now; and if you will not listen to me as I unfold this

story to you and point out to you from God's Holy Word what you will be doing and thinking the first five minutes after you are dead, you would not listen to your dead father, or mother, or a lost friend, even though they came walking out of the graveyard, with the smell of the other world upon them! If someone did come from the grave to warn you, it might cause you to quake and tremble for a little while; but you would soon explain it all away, that it was only a bad dream, or that you had seen a ghost!

It is a solemn thing to listen to the truth of God as revealed in the Bible and then not be moved by it. It is a fearful thing to refuse to take warning. It puts your own blood upon your own head, and places the whole blame of your doom upon your own soul. But I am warning you. I am telling you, sinners, how it is going to be with you the first five minutes after the breath leaves your body. May God help you to think about these things, and get right with God before death overtakes you!

II

From this glimpse into the experience of all lost souls the first five minutes after death, let us get a glimpse of the redeemed soul immediately after death. I am glad that in this same wonderful story of Dives and Lazarus we have the other side of the picture. The experience of Lazarus in this story symbolizes for us what the first five minutes after death is going to mean for every good and faithful soul. I thank God for what dear old Lazarus has meant to all sorrowing pilgrims of this sinful and suffering world.

Look at the Bible picture of Lazarus: "And there was a certain beggar named Lazarus, which was laid at his gate (the rich man's), full of sores, and desiring to be fed with the crumbs which fell from the rich man's table; moreover the dogs came and licked his sores. And it came to pass, that the beggar died, and was carried by the angels into Abraham's bosom. . . . Son (Dives), remember that thou in thy lifetime receivedst thy good things, and likewise Lazarus evil things: . . . but now he is comforted."

O my friends, that is a picture of how the poorest man in all the world may live a good life, even though he has to beg for bread; and it is a picture of how good it is going to be for all the saints of God, no matter how helpless they were here in this world, the first five minutes after they lay aside this mortal body and pass out into Paradise with all the good people of all the past.

There are several great and comforting truths suggested by this story of Lazarus:

First of all, it suggests the thought that there is no price too dear to pay for a good life. Lazarus had a hard time. He was sick, and he was poor, and practically abandoned of mankind. But he kept his heart right. He was dear in God's sight. I am certain that he wondered sometimes whether it paid to do right; and I am sure that he often wondered whether God does really care! These are questions that any man would ask, placed as Lazarus was; but, thank God, he walked by faith, and lived a good life, even though he died a pauper. Well, he shows us, first of all, that it is a million times better to live a good life, even though you die a pauper, and then go out to be with God in Paradise, than it is to live a bad life, in luxury here in the world—even if you could live that way a thousand years—and then die, and wake up in Hades! He shows us that it does really pay to do right, and that God does care for his people!

In the second place, the first five minutes after he was dead, Lazarus was out of all the sufferings, sorrows, destitution, and loneliness of this hard, sinful world! Here in this world he had had his "evil things." Over there, thank God, he "was comforted." Here in this world he had always been poor; we are not told whether he had ever had a home of his own or not, but, if he did, his folks had all forsaken him; he became a helpless invalid who had to be carried about and laid at one place or another to beg for his bread; finally, from weakness and neglect, he was all covered with great ulcers, and there was no nurse to minister to him —except the dogs that came and licked his sores! No more forlorn picture ever was painted than that! But, thank God, the first five minutes after he was dead, he was done with all his earthly ills forever, and was well, and strong, and happy! Oh, how his soul must have leaped up and praised God!

And he was in the company of all the good people who had died in faith, and there was no one in all the Paradise of God to do him harm, but to bless him, and to help him, and to join with him in praising God's name forever! If he had ever had any loved ones who had truly loved God, they were waiting for him over there. He was with Abraham, close up in his sheltering arms. That symbolizes the blessed fellowship of all the redeemed in the Paradise of God. Lazarus was one of God's aristocrats in Paradise!

But that was not all. All his life he had wondered at times just what death was going to be like. He had evidently had anxious moments about it, when his blood ran cold at the thought of dying: he had held on to life, trusting and hoping; but he had wondered about death, and dreaded it, perhaps. Who has not had such feelings? Poor Lazarus had faced this grim monster for a long time. But, at last, the first five minutes after death,—the dear old man who had had such a hard time all his life found that death was the best friend, except God, he had ever met! The fog in his throat, the mist in his face, the snows, the blast of the storm, the power of the night, were all gone! Suddenly the worst had turned best; the black minute was at an end; the rage of the elements had dwindled, blended, changed; first there was peace out of pain, then light, then Abraham's bosom, and rest with God! He had learned that death is not to be feared by God's children. Oh, how wonderful it was!

And, again, we are told here that when he died— when dear old Lazarus died—"he was carried by the *angels* into Abraham's bosom." What does that mean? Why it means, my friends, that none of God's children ever die alone! God sends his angels to stand by them, and to help them in that last struggle, and to escort them up the shining slopes of the skies to the Paradise of God, where they lay aside every burden forever, and where they begin their endless bliss with the redeemed. I am so glad that dear old Lazarus had such a happy entrance into Paradise! All this should take the sting out of death for all God's children, for in the last great struggle that we call death, God gives us a band of angels to minister to us; and none of God's servants ever die in loneliness! As friends on this side do their last ministries of love, our angelic escort takes up the task, and carries us away to our immortal Home.

Victor Hugo, in his great story of Jean Valjean, pictures the old man at the end of his long life. He had suffered more than almost any of the sons of men; but he had loved his little adopted daughter, Cosette, and her young husband. He had lived for her; he wanted to help her; he had meant everything to her, and he had managed so that she and Marius, her husband whom he had also saved from death, were happy. And now he was dying—and they have come to be with him! He says: "So I am going away, my children. Love each other dearly always. There is scarcely anything else in the world but that—to love one another. . . . Cosette and Marius fell on their knees overwhelmed, choked with tears, each grasping one of Jean Valjean's hands. Those august hands moved no more. He had fallen backward, the light from the candlesticks fell upon him; his white face looked up towards heaven; he let Cosette and Marius cover his hands with kisses; he was dead. The night was starless and very dark. *Without doubt, in the gloom some mighty angel was standing with outstretched wings, awaiting the soul.*" That is precisely what happens to every faithful soul; when the great separation takes place and the soul goes on its long journey, thank God, it does not go alone! There is always an angel escort to convey all of God's

children to Abraham's bosom—to the glorified th
in the Paradise of God.

Now, Lazarus—poor Lazarus—realized the first five
minutes after death the glory and reality of Paradise,
as contrasted with the sorrows and sufferings of this
present world.

Orison Swett Marden, for a long time editor of *Success,* an inspirational magazine for young people, and
the author of many books, was once a sort of hero to me.
He was a remarkable man. But he never knew what
his name was, or where he came from. As a child he
was taken in by a family by the name of Marden, but
he never knew anything about his parents. So when
he grew to young manhood, he became a devout Christian, and became ambitious to make his life a blessing
to all young people, and especially to those who were unfortunate, or who needed encouragement. Not having
any name, after he grew up *he named himself,* taking
the symbolic name Orison Swett Marden, the name suggesting prayer and sweat. Those two words constituted
his philosophy of life: he believed that one could do
anything that God wanted him to do, if he was willing
to pray and sweat enough about it!

Heaven only will reveal how many thousands of
young people lighted the fires of their ambition at the
altar of this man's courage and purpose. But the point
of this story is this: Mr. Marden always cherished
the hope that in the world ahead, which was so real
to him, he would find out some of the secrets that had
been hidden from him all his life. He had almost a
childish curiosity to know about his father and mother;
and never till the end of his life did he cease to wonder

about the mystery of his own identity. He lived a saintly life, and when he was dying, he smiled and said to his loved ones: "It is real!—It is real!—just as I have always hoped and believed it would be! It is all beautiful!" And with a smile on his face, he passed over to the other side.

The first five minutes after death we shall know that our hopes as God's children were not in vain; we shall know that God did not fool us when he planted the hope of a blessed immortality in our hearts! It will even be better, I think, than we had hoped or dreamed!

So, in conclusion, I have two words of appeal. First, I want to urge you, Christians, to be faithful. It will not be long till we shall be through with our labors here. It will be but a few years at most. If you have grown cold, or discouraged, think of Lazarus. No man ever had a harder lot in life than he had, or more discouragement; but he remained faithful, and died in the Lord! And when he came down to death, and passed on to the other side, I am sure that he felt that the rewards over there were worth a thousand lifetimes of struggle such as he had here. I am sure he felt that, if he had to repeat this life a thousand times, enduring the same privations and sufferings over and over for a thousand times, it would be worth all the sufferings that it would entail, just to be at last at home with God forever! If you have wandered away, if you have weakened in your devotion to Christ and to the church, come back tonight; renew your vows, and resolve to be faithful till death. May God help you to do this!

And to you who are not Christians, I want to appeal to you to give your hearts to Christ tonight. Don't make the mistake that Dives made! As I intimated a little while ago, probably Dives expected to attend to this matter before he died. But he waited till it was too late! Sinner friends, don't make that mistake! Accept Christ as your Saviour tonight. May God help you to do this right now!

X

THE CONCLUSION OF THE WHOLE MATTER

Let us hear the conclusion of the whole matter: Fear God, and keep his commandments: for this is the whole duty of man.—ECCLESIASTES 12: 13.

I speak to you this morning from Ecclesiastes 12: 13, "Let us hear the conclusion of the whole matter: fear God, and keep his commandments: for this is the whole duty of man."

I think this is the greatest verse in the Old Testament because it gives us the clue to the enduring satisfactions of life, and sums up for us the whole duty of man. It contains the irreducible essence of the wisdom of mankind with regard to the baffling problems of life here in the world. It gives us in two brief injunctions a practical philosophy of life which comprehends our whole duty.

I

The writer of this text was a great philosopher; he was conceded to be the wisest man of his day. His purpose was to find out first-hand what is "good for man to do all the days of his life." He says that he "set himself to search and investigate in wisdom everything that is done beneath the heavens." Although he lived in pre-scientific times, he, nevertheless, used the scientific method. He was a great experimenter with life. He resolved to find out by trial and error what is good for man. He and Browning seem to have had the same

[150]

point of view. Browning said: "Life has meaning, and to find its meaning is my meat and drink." This quest for the ultimate meaning of life has always been "the dear delight," as Plato says, of all thoughtful souls. It was the purpose of the writer of our text.

With such an attitude, he threw aside all conventions, and using his kingly freedom, as a true and untrammeled liberal, he tested life to see what was worth while.

First, he tried wisdom and the pursuit of knowledge on the purely human level, to see if enduring satisfaction lay in the quest of knowledge. In this he was wonderfully successful, for he won for himself the name of being the wisest man that had ever lived. Most of us would have felt that that was quite a success. But what did Solomon say about it? He felt, though he had followed "knowledge beyond the utmost bound of human thought," that it was only "following a sinking star." He says, "I gave my heart to seek and search out by wisdom concerning all things that are under heaven: . . . Lo, I . . . have gotten more wisdom than all they that have been before me in Jerusalem: yea, my heart had great experience of wisdom and knowledge. And I . . . perceive that this also is vexation of spirit. For in much wisdom is much grief: And he that increaseth knowledge increaseth sorrow."

Then he tried "madness and folly" to see if enduring satisfaction lay in that direction. He threw God and all restraints aside, and plunged into a life of unrestrained dissipation. You can see how he reasoned about it: he had tried wisdom and prudence on the purely human level, and they had not given satisfaction; so he swung to the other extreme—to "madness and folly." He had tried the life of the godless philosopher, and had found no key to happiness; now he would try the life of the libertine. He said to himself: "Come now and let me try you (life) with mirth, so enjoy yourself." But that also was vanity! In his experiment of madness and folly he tried everything that he could think of from "the stimulation of drink" to the last invention of the giddy round of worldly dissipation. His purpose was serious, however; he was trying to find out "what is good for men to practice all the days of their life." And what was the outcome of his experiment with "madness and folly"? Did he find enduring satisfaction in such a course? Not at all! Although he had failed to find satisfaction in the pursuit of knowledge, it had yielded him more pleasure than "madness and folly": for his conclusion as to this wild experiment was—

> Wisdom is more profitable than folly,
> Even as light is preferable to darkness.

But failing to find satisfaction in the pursuit of wisdom and of folly, he next went in for great works. He built mansions and planted vineyards, laid out gardens and parks in which he planted all kinds of trees, made irrigation systems to water the trees in his plantations; he bought slaves, both men and women, and had slaves born in his household; he had large herds and flocks, larger than any before him in Jerusalem; he amassed silver and gold, and great royal treasures; he secured men singers and women singers, and mistresses for himself from many lands. Richer and richer he grew, more than any before him in Jerusalem. Nothing he desired did he deny himself, nor did his wisdom fail him, he says (Eccl. 3). Now, some of us have imagined that we would be happy if we could lead such a life as that. But did Solomon find satisfaction in that kind of life? No; he did not! Here is what he said about it: "And I reviewed all my works which my hands had made and the toil which I had expended in making them, and, lo; everything was a futility and striving after wind, and there was no profit in it under the sun" (Eccl. 2: 11—Goodspeed). And so his experimentation led him just where it leads all men and women who have sold themselves for silver and gold, and the things that silver and gold can buy!

II

And so, after searching everywhere under the sun for "that which is good for men to practice all the days of his life," the writer of our text says: "Let us hear the conclusion of the whole matter: fear God, and keep his commandments: for this is the whole duty of man." He had discovered that he had been looking in the wrong places for enduring satisfaction. This man's experience is God's flood-light upon the baffling problem of human life. We would do well to accept these conclusions of this wise man in practically the same way that we accept the discoveries of the great scientists, like Euclid, Copernicus, Sir Isaac Newton, Pasteur, and all the rest who have planted mile-posts along the road of human progress. This is one of the great conclusions of human experience that we can accept as the very truth of God.

Let us, therefore, reverently ponder the two injunctions of this text. They hold within their brief compass "the whole duty of man."

First, "Fear God." What does that mean? Over in Kentucky a few years ago a little girl had as her memory verse in her Sunday school lesson that gem from Proverbs, "The fear of the Lord is the beginning of wisdom." When her teacher asked her to repeat it, she said: "Getting scared of God is the beginning of smartness." Well, some of us never get much further with our understanding of "the fear of the Lord" than the little girl did; but it has a great deal more in it for us than just "getting scared of God."

The Bible never attempts to prove the existence of God; it always assumes his existence. His existence as Creator and Preserver is the prime assumption of the Scriptures, and "to fear God" implies our acceptance of this great assumption, namely: that God is. But in case there should be some here who have had doubts about God, I remind you that your doubts need not be sinful. It is not sinful to think about God, and we cannot think much about God without raising questions. It is an old, old battlefield of the philosophers and theologians; but if one thinks long enough and deep enough about God, he will come to the conclusion that it is immeasurably more reasonable to believe in the existence of God than it is to disbelieve.

Solomon, the wisest of the Bible philosophers, had to admit after a long life of thought about God, that he could not "trace out the ways of God from beginning to end"; and if Solomon felt that way, we need not become discouraged over our partial knowledge about him. If we are to lose faith in everything we do not fully understand, we will lose faith in everything. The main reason for doubting God's existence on the part of those who call themselves atheists seems to be that they cannot see him with their eyes. Well, they cannot see the wind, but they know it blows; they cannot see ether, nor electricity; but they make use of them. Think of the marvels of radio. When the music is on the air we do not see the notes of the violin as they are blown over the mountains or over the city's din, but we know they come to us and in our receiving sets are converted into sounds; we cannot see the songs as they are tossed over the continent and sea, but we know that with our receiving sets we can "cull them like fragrant roses from the thin blue air" and enjoy them. And then we know there is an artist and a broadcasting station somewhere. We use means of manifesting ourselves, and God uses means for manifesting himself. We cannot understand God fully, neither can we understand radio fully, nor electricity, nor gravitation, nor the "flower in the crannied wall," nor life itself. But we know that all these things are among the great realities of our everyday experiences. And since we do accept these mysteries and make use of them even though we do not understand them, I think Bulwer-Lytton was right when he said:

> There is no doubt;
> Whoever plants a seed beneath the sod,
> And waits to see it push away the clod,
> He trusts in God.
> Whosoever says, when clouds are in the sky,
> "Be patient, heart; light breaketh by and by,"
> Trusts the Most High.

Whoever sees, 'neath winter's fields of snow,
The silent harvest of the future grow,
God's power must know.
Whoever lies down on his couch to sleep,
Content to lock each sense in slumber deep,
Knows God will keep.
There is no unbelief;
And day by day, and night unconsciously,
The heart lives by that faith the lips deny.

To fear God implies belief in his existence and belief in his authority. Rebellion against God has always been one of the besetting sins of mankind. It was flouting God's authority that led Adam in the Garden of Eden to partake of the forbidden fruit. But I wonder if we today realize that this old sin of rebellion against God is the most rampant sin in the world. Most of us have lost the sense of God's authority in our lives. Back in the days of the Judges, the Bible tells us: "every man did that which was right in his own eyes," and because they did so, that period of Israel's history became the "Dark Age" of the Old Testament. In our day there is such a spirit of rebellion against God that it seems we are plunging again into a dark age of infidelity and atheism. Our Bibles have lost their validity as God's Word for our lives; we read them and then either ridicule them, or else ignore them; the church has lost its authority; for we neither listen to its admonitions nor take account of its bands; the very idea of God has been so widely questioned that it is becoming "stylish" to profess atheism, and to live as if God were an outgrown myth of an age of superstition and ignorance. We no longer recognize God's authority to command, or his right to be obeyed!

Recently a professor in one of our colleges was called to the pastorate of one of our large churches. On his first Sunday as pastor, he preached from the memorable words of Peter and the rest of the apostles when they refused to stop preaching in the name of Christ: "We ought to obey God rather than man." More than a hundred converts flocked down the aisles of the church that morning in response to that sermon, confessing Christ and uniting with the church. That pastor was asked later why he gave up a place as professor in a great college to become pastor of a church. His reply was: "We ought to obey God rather than man." My friends, we ought to recognize God's authority in our lives. It is essential to any great living. It is a great part of the fear of God.

Daniel Webster was asked on one occasion what was the most solemn thought that ever entered his mind; he replied: "The most solemn thought that ever entered my mind is the thought of my individual accountability to God." I have a feeling that that is the most solemn thought that ever entered the mind of any man. And it brings before us another aspect of the fear of God; it brings before us the fact of the great Judgment-seat of Christ.

Somehow, it has crept over humanity like a slow paralysis that we can treat God with scorn and contempt with absolute impunity; that we can defy him to his face and escape the consequences of our perversity; that we can break every one of God's commandments and never give an account of ourselves to God at all. But, my friends, in all this we are totally wrong! If there is any law in the universe more thoroughly attested than all others it is the law that sin brings sorrow. We cannot sin and escape the consequences of our doing; we must reap what we sow; we must give an account of ourselves to God, whether our deeds be good or evil! That is a law that we see operative in all the world, which must hold good in all worlds! Immediately after our text with its great admonition, Solomon, as if to give this text cogency and force, says: "For God will bring every work into judgment, with every hidden thing, whether it be good, or whether it be evil." This great and solemn thought of the final Judgment runs through the entire Bible, and stood as the key-stone in the arch of the teachings of all the New Testament writers. In Matthew 25: 31-46, Christ gives his own matchless picture of this great and final settlement with every soul according to his works; there the righteous and the wicked are to be finally and eternally separated, the one from the other, as a shepherd separates the sheep from the goats. The Judgment stands as God's constant reminder to each and every soul in the universe of its eternal and inescapable accountability to the Almighty. Without the Judgment and without a righteous and reigning God back of it, there would be no regard for good and evil; there could be no feeling of right and wrong; no merit or demerit; no sense of duty nor the fear of punishment. Without Judgment to come, men lose their fear of God. But I remind you that a vast part of "the fear of God" is born in our hearts as we remind ourselves that we must stand before him to give an account of ourselves to him, whether our deeds be good, or whether they be evil!

When we realize that God is real, and that he has absolute authority over us, and that we shall shortly stand before him to give an account of ourselves, we can see that we should walk reverently and humbly before him. We can see that we should be afraid to treat him with contempt. God will not be mocked. We should love him, and seek to walk humbly before him. We should seek at all times to acknowledge him in all our ways. All this is comprehended in the injunction, "Fear God."

III

Notice briefly the second injunction: "Keep his commandments." Keeping God's commandments is the natural consequence of "fearing God." Here we come to the practical side of our religion. The first injunction of our text has to do with our attitude towards God, the faith side, the reverence and respect side of our relationship to God. The second injunction has to do with the practical side of our relationship to God. I remind you, therefore, that "faith without works is dead"; and, by the same token, I remind you that a religion that does not make us good and does not make us *do good* is not worth having. A religion that saves us changes us; it makes us willing and anxious to keep God's commandments!

This is the significance of this second part of our text. In effect, it says: "You say you fear God; well, prove it by keeping his commandments!" The only way we can prove that we fear God, that we love God, that we believe in God, that we have the right attitude toward God, is by obeying him, which means keeping his commandments. Jesus said: "If you love me, you will keep my commandments." And again he said, "Why call ye me Lord, Lord, and do not the things which I say?" and in another place he says: "Not every one that saith unto me, Lord, Lord, shall enter into the kingdom of heaven; but he that doeth the will of my Father who is in heaven." And when he had preached the Sermon on the Mount, he urged his hearers to do the things he had taught them. He said, "Whosoever heareth these sayings of mine and doeth them, I will liken him unto a wise man, which built his house upon a rock: and every one that heareth these sayings of mine, and doeth them not, shall be likened unto a foolish man, which built his house upon the sand: . . . and the rain descended, and the floods came, and the winds blew and beat upon that house; and it fell: and great was the fall of it." But the house of the wise man stood, "because it was founded upon a rock." The difference in those two men was that one heard the words of Christ, and did nothing about it; while the other heard, and proceeded to put into practice what he heard.

Just so, when our text says, "Keep his commandments," it means that we must do what we know is good to do; we must be more than hearers; we must live our religion! It means that we must "prove our faith by our works," or else our faith will be proved to be dead, and therefore worthless!

This is my message to you from this great Old Testament text. May God add his blessing to his word. "Let us hear the conclusion of the whole matter: fear God, and keep his commandments: for this is the whole duty of man."